S0-AZI-800

Women and Folklore

Women and Folklore

Edited by Claire R. Farrer

University of Texas Press

Austin and London

International Standard Book Number 0–292–79005–8 (cloth);
0–292–79006–6 (paper)
Library of Congress Catalog Card Number 76–14078
Copyright © 1975 by the American Folklore Society
All rights reserved
Printed in the United States of America

Previously published in *Journal of American Folklore* 88,
no. 347 (January–March 1975).

Contents

Introduction

Women and Folklore: Images and Genres

CLAIRE R. FARRER

FOLKLORISTS HAVE LONG PAID LIP SERVICE to the importance of women's expressive behavior, though usually that behavior was recognized and accorded legitimacy only when it occurred in predetermined genres that fit the prevailing image of women. Beginning folklore students learn that the brothers Grimm collected primarily from women servants and relatives in the early 1800's.[1] The JOURNAL OF AMERICAN FOLKLORE in 1899 published a bibliography of women's folklore.[2] Mark Azadovskii in 1926 presented a study of a female storyteller that focused on her creativity and expressive behavior.[3] Ruth L. Bunzel indicated the interplay of form and personal creativity among women artisans in the Southwestern Pueblos.[4] Zora Neale Hurston described black women's speech styles and individual strategies of verbal manipulation within the context of an autobiographical novel.[5]

Thus, folklore scholarship pertaining to women is not a new concern, as a survey of the JOURNAL from its 1888 inception also indicates.[6] During the 1880's and 1890's women's expressive behavior was believed to be manifest in charms, quaint customs and beliefs, home remedies, and some retelling of folktales. In this latter instance, when a collector had a choice between a story as told by a man or as told by a woman, the man's version was chosen.[7]

In the first decade of the twentieth century the preponderance of items concerning women were witch stories from black, Indian, Anglo, and Spanish-American perspectives. During the second decade most articles in the JOURNAL concerning women (other than as characters in stories or songs) featured a play-party theme. Women, as well as men, contributed collectanea usually entitled "The Folk-Lore of ————," the blank being filled by the name of an Indian tribe, a community, a county, a state, or a country. Sometimes women informants were cited, but women seem to have been consulted only if male informants were unavailable or if the material concerned an area thought of as women's prerogative.

The swinging, liberated 1920's had many more articles written by women, but

---

[1] Murray B. Peppard, *Paths through the Forest: A Biography of the Brothers Grimm* (New York, 1971), 50–51.

[2] Isabel Cushman Chamberlain, "Contributions Toward a Bibliography of Folk-Lore Relating to Women," JOURNAL OF AMERICAN FOLKLORE, 12 (1899), 32–37.

[3] *A Siberian Tale Teller*, trans. James R. Dow, Folklore Fellows Communications No. 68 (Helsinki, 1926).

[4] *The Pueblo Potter* (New York, 1929).

[5] Zora Neale Hurston, *Mules and Men* (Philadelphia, 1935).

[6] See Claire R. Farrer and Susan J. Kalčik, "Women: A Selected Bibliography from the *Journal of American Folklore*, 1888–1973," *Folklore Feminists Communication*, 1 (1973), 12–28.

[7] See, for example, W. W. Beauchamp, "Onondaga Tales," JOURNAL OF AMERICAN FOLKLORE, 1 (1888), 44–48.

few of these actually concerned women or used women as informants. Those that did dealt, by and large, with play-parties and beliefs.

The 1930's were particularly impoverished in terms of data on women: during the entire decade the JOURNAL had only six articles dealing with women's lore or women's expressive culture. The 1940's were little better: twelve articles, two of which were obituaries and one a book review, concerned women, their lore, or expressive activities.

In the early 1950's, more than double the number of articles relating to women were published than had appeared in the entirety of the previous two decades. This trend continued through the 1950's and into the 1960's. However, the articles still were overwhelmingly biased toward charms, marriage customs, and birth practices, though occasional articles featured the roles of women in various societies.

In the 1970's, articles still concerned folk beliefs of women, charms women use, and women's roles, but newer themes such as verse competitions and stereotypes of women were introduced as well. Nonetheless the general trend throughout the history of the JOURNAL has been to rely on data from women for information about health, charms, some games, and various beliefs and customs but in other areas to use women as informants only when men informants were unavailable.

This journal was not the only one following such a course. Similar patterns appear in regional publications, such as the Texas Folklore Society publications or California's *Western Folklore*. The trend is also evident in collections like *The Frank C. Brown Collection of North Carolina Folklore* or Archer Taylor's *English Riddles from Oral Tradition*, as well as the W.P.A. Writers' Project *Gumbo Ya-Ya*.[8]

The paucity of women's folkloristic data during the 1930's in the JOURNAL is mirrored in the lack of concern with women's subjects in books and articles during the 1940's and 1950's. The 1940's were an era of culture-at-a-distance studies in which whole cultures were examined. Some of the parameters investigated (child-rearing practices, for example) perforce concerned women, but emphasis was on the culture rather than on the beliefs and customs characterizing subgroups within the culture. Few studies examined similarities or differences between male and female expressive behavior, though there was widespread familiarity both with Margaret Mead's illustration of how society molds men and women within it and with Gregory Bateson's characterization of ethos and the differences between the separate belief systems and behavior of Iatmul men and women.[9]

Little of significance relating to women's folklore was published during the

---

[8] Newman Ivey White, ed., *The Frank C. Brown Collection of North Carolina Folklore* (Durham, North Carolina, 1952); Archer Taylor, *English Riddles from Oral Tradition* (Berkeley, 1951); Lyle Saxon, Edward Dreyer, and Robert Tallant, eds., *Gumbo Ya-Ya* (New York, 1945).

[9] Margaret Mead, *Sex and Temperament in Three Primitive Societies* (first published, 1935; New York, 1963); Gregory Bateson, *Naven* (first published, 1936; 2nd ed.: Stanford, 1958), especially chaps. 9 and 10.

1950's, but it was a period of rather intensive fieldwork, some of which concerned women and resulted in studies published in the 1960's. Francis Lambrecht focused on a genre, the *hudhúd*, performed by women in the Philippines.[10] He described presentation, composition, and chorus performances of these lengthy, sung narratives, as well as differences in expression of them during actual performance conditions and dictation of texts. Linda Dégh's investigation of Hungarian folktales and their tellers, while primarily concerned with men, discussed women storytellers as well; she considered reasons for the general lack of public performances by women and aspects of their creativity and individual style.[11]

More recently, Roger Abrahams has examined in detail the style, repertoire, and conscious manipulation of elements producing the songs performed by a female singer.[12] Both Robbie Davis Johnson and Beverly Stoeltje have investigated women's usage of verbal resources to control interactional situations.[13] Bessie Jones and Bess Lomax Hawes have worked from the bottom up, as it were, by looking at black girls' play behavior for information regarding children's and adults' styles of movement, outlook, and expectations of others.[14]

Feminist literature from Simone de Beauvoir to Shulamith Firestone espouses the cause of exploding the contemporary "myths" of women being by nature secondary and servile to men.[15] These myths are seen as man germinated and man cultivated but as accepted by most women—albeit reluctantly.

The consciousness of men as well as of women was raised by feminist literature, and this led to the current revival of interest in women's rights in all areas of life. The literature and polemics have focused attention on our images of women, and academic disciplines have not been immune to the feminist impact. Thus the historian Ronald Hogeland notes that fellow historians have made women either invisible or absurd by defining women's roles on the basis of men's attitudes; Rae Carlson echoes this position but from a sociological perspective.[16] Using statistics on women factory workers in the mid-nineteenth century, Gerda Lerner attacks the myth that post-colonial American women were hearth-bound, while Marija Matich Hughes explores some problems feminists

---

[10] "The *Hudhúd* of Dinulawan and Bugan at Gonhadan," *Saint Louis Quarterly*, 5 (1967), 267–713.

[11] *Folktales and Society*, trans. Emily M. Schossberger (Bloomington, Indiana, 1969).

[12] *A Singer and Her Songs: Almeda Riddle's Book of Ballads* (Baton Rouge, 1970); see also his "Creativity, Individuality, and the Traditional Singer," *Studies in the Literary Imagination*, 3 (1970), 5–34.

[13] Robbie Davis Johnson, "Folklore and Women: A Social Interactional Analysis of the Folklore of a Texas Madam," JOURNAL OF AMERICAN FOLKLORE, 86 (1973), 211–224; Beverly J. Stoeltje, "Bow-legged Bastard: 'A Manner of Speaking' Speech Behavior of a Black Woman," *Folklore Annual*, 4 and 5 (1973), 152–178.

[14] *Step It Down* (New York, 1972).

[15] Simone de Beauvoir, *The Second Sex*, trans. and ed. H. M. Parshley (first published, 1949; New York, 1970); Shulamith Firestone, *The Dialectic of Sex* (New York, 1972). I use *myth* in de Beauvoir's sense; see especially *The Second Sex*, xxv, xxix, and chap. 1 of Book I.

[16] Ronald W. Hogeland, "The Female Appendage: Feminine Life-Styles in America, 1820–1860," *Civil War History*, 17 (1971), 101–114; Rae Carlson, "Understanding Women: Implications for Personality Theory and Research," *Journal of Social Issues*, 18 (1972), 217–231.

have today in trying to operate as liberated women in a sexist law system.[17] Similar voices are heard in other disciplines within the social and behavioral sciences.

Today, opinion concerning scholarship devoted to women's behavior is divided. On the one hand are those who proclaim that women's studies and studies of women and their interests are new, a product of the feminist movement; on the other are those who see scholarship concerning women as having a long, pedigreed history. As is often the case with such dichotomies, both views are simultaneously correct. If the journals and other publications surveyed above, as well as the historical trends outlined, represent reality, then women's creativity and expressive behavior have been limited to home and hearth activities until rather recently. This conclusion is inevitable given the prevailing image of women and the description of women's folklore wholly within a priori genres. The feminists have engendered a new emphasis and impetus for the study of women. But scholarship, and in particular folklore scholarship, has not totally ignored the question of women's creativity and expressiveness.

Though the majority of folklore studies and folklorists have viewed women's expressiveness and creativity in restricted, a priori categories, a consistent thread of investigative scholarship has suggested that the predetermined genres and generally accepted images of women are not the only ones valid for describing women or their folklore. The works previously cited of Abrahams, Azadovskii, Dégh, Johnson, and Stoeltje come immediately to mind. In some cultures certain tools are used by only one sex;[18] in other cultures certain expressive forms are sex-specific, that is, women are excluded from some of men's expressive events and men are prohibited from some of women's expressive activities. In Iraq a man's presence is enough to terminate a miming event among women.[19] In Morocco men are ignorant of a body of women's folklore that comes into play only when women are together; any males present are such small children that they do not remember the events or acts when they are adults.[20] The a priori categories do indeed have validity, but it is a mistake to assume that these are the *only* valid genres.

Some situations and settings are recognized both etically and emically as appropriate for women to perform in, just as there are those situations and settings in which it is appropriate for men to perform. The general-store setting described by Richard Bauman is one of these male settings, as is the street corner discussed by Ulf Hannerz.[21] Each of these is a setting where men are in groups

---

[17] Gerda Lerner, "The Lady and the Mill Girl: Changes in the Status of Women in the Age of Jackson," *American Studies*, 10 (1969), 5–15; Marija Matich Hughes, "And Then There Were Two," *The Hastings Law Journal*, 23 (1971), 233–247.

[18] Lois Paul, "Work and Sex in a Guatemalan Village," in *Women, Culture, and Society*, ed. Michelle Zimbalist Rosaldo and Louise Lamphere (Stanford, 1974), 284.

[19] Elizabeth Warnock Fernea, *Guests of the Sheik* (New York, 1969), 327.

[20] Fernea, personal communication.

[21] Richard Bauman, "The La Have Island General Store: Sociability and Verbal Art in a Nova Scotia Community," JOURNAL OF AMERICAN FOLKLORE, 85 (1972), 330–343; Ulf Hannerz, *Soulside* (New York, 1969), especially chap. 5.

with other men for sociability purposes, in Georg Simmel's sense of that term, that is, they are gathered together for the pleasure it brings and for the interactions that result.[22]

Yet at least half of the expressive repertoire of a society is overlooked by investigating only the verbal or expressive behavior of one sex or those areas where one sex performs. The folk are not at fault for suppression of half the relevant data; folklorists, and other collectors, must accept the responsibility for bias. Still we continue our fictions.

Consider, for example, the early work in the JOURNAL. Men knew the beliefs women had, or were said to have, just as men today know many women believe it will make them sick to wash their hair during menstruation. But we have no data concerning what beliefs men of that time had or how men or women actually utilized their beliefs. I am not suggesting we stop collecting beliefs from women; I *am* suggesting we collect also from men and consider the attitudes of both men and women toward our collectanea. Further, I am suggesting that we no longer base our theories, hypothetical constructs, and models on half of the available data. Because the other half of the data is more difficult to reach is no reason to ignore it.

Men's activities usually take place in public arenas, women's in more private ones. As Edwin Ardner noted, "surface structure may express the male view of the world, obscuring the existence at deeper levels of an autonomous female view."[23] Thus, Hannerz found men talking on street corners and Bauman found them talking in a general store, whereas Fernea found women talking behind walls and closed doors. Stoeltje found women's talk performances in homes among friends.[24] Claudia Mitchell-Kernan found female correlates to men's speech (long recognized as performance) both in the home and in mixed-group interaction outside the home.[25]

Because the public arenas are more readily accessible than private ones, it is too often assumed they are the dominant, if not the only, areas where expressive activity occurs. William Ferris succumbs to this trap.[26] After stating that he "collected primarily from males," he continues, "in folklore sessions . . . women never participated unless encouraged by the men present"; he acknowledges that "if past folklore studies of prose narrative had been done by women rather than men, an extensive 'feminine' tradition . . . might have been recorded."[27] Yet he ignores the implications of his own statements by concluding, "We can say with certainty that the dominant or primary oral tradition among Delta blacks is male, and that females rarely participate in sessions involving either

[22] *The Sociology of Georg Simmel*, ed. and trans. Kurt H. Wolff (first published in English, 1950; New York, 1964), 52.

[23] "Belief and the Problem of Women," in *The Interpretation of Ritual*, ed. J. S. LaFontaine (London, 1972), 152.

[24] Stoeltje, *passim*.

[25] "Signifying and Marking: Two Afro-American Speech Acts," in *Directions in Sociolinguistics*, ed. John J. Gumperz and Dell Hymes (New York, 1972), 161–179.

[26] William R. Ferris, Jr., "Black Prose Narratives in the Mississippi Delta," JOURNAL OF AMERICAN FOLKLORE, 85 (1972), 140–151.

[27] Ibid., 141.

blues or prose narrative."[28] We can say no such thing with certainty. We *can* say with certainty that Delta black females rarely perform among Delta black males when a white male collector is present, even if the setting is a private home. I have not seen data that support—or refute—Ferris' position; he has simply generalized beyond his data by basing his conclusions on half of the population. Until female collectors, and preferably black female collectors, discover the range of Delta black women's expressive activities and the material included in them, statements such as Ferris' about primary or dominant traditions must be considered premature and ill-advised at best.

R. D. Laing states that "the attributes one ascribes to a person define him and put him in a particular position. By assigning him to a particular position, attributions 'put him in his place' and thus have in effect the force of injunctions."[29] Defining woman as not man automatically excludes her from man's world and man's concerns. A general-store storytelling session is a place where woman does not belong. That is not to say that she does not go to the general store; she does, of course, but only for instrumental, not social, purposes. Nor is it to say she is unfamiliar with the general-store story genre, with its attendant rules for production and performance; it is only to say she is enjoined from participating in the storytelling talk that occurs in the general store. Again quoting Laing, "Insofar as we experience the world differently, in a sense we live in different worlds."[30] The general store exists as a locality for both men and women. But that locality represents entirely different expected behavior patterns for the two sexes: the general store is two different worlds, depending upon the persons present and their reasons for being there at a given time.

According to Kenneth Boulding, *"behavior depends on the image"* [italics his].[31] As I have briefly outlined, the image of women dominant in American folkloristics is one of creatures confined to home and hearth, conversant with charms and cures and possessing various quaint beliefs. At times woman was seen as a danger, a witch; other times she was a frivolous child interested in games. She may have known and bequeathed a rich traditional heritage, but information is sketchy concerning the extent of her folklore repertoire. Her image was that of homebody; her behavior, even in areas outside the home, was consistent with her image.

When women wrote scholarly articles their subjects were limited to natural phenomena, games, or things associated with the home.[32] Occasionally a woman would contribute an article to this journal concerning an ethnic group's folk-

---

[28] Ibid., 142.

[29] *Self and Others*, 2nd ed. (New York, 1971), 151.

[30] Ibid., 37.

[31] *The Image* (Ann Arbor, 1973), 6.

[32] See for instance Fanny D. Bergen and W. W. Newell, "Weather Lore," JOURNAL OF AMERICAN FOLKLORE, 2 (1889), 203–208; Fanny Bergen, "Some Saliva Charms," JOURNAL OF AMERICAN FOLKLORE, 3 (1890), 51–59; Mary Olmsted Clarke, "Song Games of Negro Children in Virginia," JOURNAL OF AMERICAN FOLKLORE, 3 (1890), 288–290; Fanny D. Bergen, "Popular American Plant Names," JOURNAL OF AMERICAN FOLKLORE, 5 (1892), 89–106; Jane H. Newell, "Superstitions of Irish Origin in Boston, Mass.," JOURNAL OF AMERICAN FOLKLORE, 5 (1892), 242–243; and Alice Morse Earle, "Old-Time Marriage Customs in New England," JOURNAL OF AMERICAN FOLKLORE, 6 (1893), 97–102.

lore,[33] but this was rare until the days of the women scholars who trained under Boas. Taylor stated the situation as it existed for a long time with the remark that, if it could be seen from a kitchen window, it was woman's domain.[34]

Not all women tacitly accepted their assigned image. Many used humor to attack the stereotypes of their ascribed role and status.[35] Women stitched onto samplers sardonic references to their image, as may sometimes be found in museums.[36] Men, too, utilized humor to question the prevailing image of women.[37]

De Beauvoir wrote that woman "is defined and differentiated with reference to man . . . she is the incidental, the inessential as opposed to the essential. He is Subject, he is Absolute—she is the Other."[38] She expounds on the concept of woman as Other throughout her book as she discusses women's reasons for accepting Other status, their incorporation of that status into their own cognitive view of Self, and the necessity of having an Other against which to define Self.[39] Laing continues this line of thought and states that Other is, simply, not Self.[40]

The image of women as Other has been a constraining influence on women. That image has also had an analogous effect on some men who have limited themselves and their insights by accepting the image unquestioned. Unfortunately, the constraint is in operation now as it was in the past. It is easier, however, to accept Beauchamp's refusal to consider seriously a woman storyteller in 1888 than it is to accept the contemporary situation Dell Hymes described where a collector recently destroyed tapes when he learned that the stories a woman had told him were not "traditional" but were of her own creation.[41] Though this image of women has had deleterious effects on scholarship, it still has intellectual currency.

Much has been written about men in groups, including Lionel Tiger's recent book by that name.[42] Whatever its demerits and delusions, the book does make the point that there is—and probably always has been—a sexual division of labor such that men are grouped with men. Women, then, are grouped with other women and with small children both male and female: women's hearth and home activities involve not only other women but also children of both sexes. It does not matter how or why these women and children groups are constituted,

[33] For example, Mary Chapman, "Notes on the Chinese in Boston," JOURNAL OF AMERICAN FOLKLORE, 5 (1892), 321–324.

[34] Taylor, 5.

[35] For a discussion of humor in writings and drawings of nineteenth-century women, see Martha Bensley Bruère and Mary Ritter Beard, eds., Laughing Their Way: Women's Humor in America (New York, 1934).

[36] Ibid., 294.

[37] For some examples see Mody C. Boatright, Folk Laughter on the American Frontier (New York, 1961).

[38] De Beauvoir, xvi.

[39] Ibid., xvii, xxi, xxv, 43, 46, 53, 63, 65, 73, 133, 261, 372.

[40] Laing, passim.

[41] "The 'Wife' Who 'Goes Out' Like a Man: Reinterpretation of a Clackamas Chinook Myth," in Structural Analysis of Oral Tradition, ed. Pierre Maranda and Elli Köngäs Maranda (Philadelphia, 1971), 52.

[42] Men in Groups (New York, 1970).

nor does it matter what historical precedents originally shaped the groups. There are, however, other interesting questions. What happens, folkloristically, in such women-oriented groups? Is the behavior the same or different from that found in mixed groups or in groups of men? How do women's experiences as children shape their expressive options as adults? What are the cultural variables influencing the range of expressive and creative activities available to women? How are a culture's perceptions of women and expectations of them expressed folkloristically? How has the implicit cultural view of women been utilized in the mass media? How have historical forces within our own discipline colored our perceptions of women's expressive experiences? More succinctly, just what are the parameters of women's folklore and on which images are they predicated?

Obviously, these questions cannot be answered satisfactorily in a few paragraphs or pages. Complete answers will require interdisciplinary research. We have begun to ask the questions; this issue of the JOURNAL begins to provide some of the answers by examining both the images of women and the genres through which women's creativity has been viewed and by suggesting genres and approaches not previously recognized.[43]

Each of the articles in this issue deals with women and their images as seen by themselves and others. In some of them, of course, images are a more central concern than in others. Beverly Stoeltje writes on images of frontier women. Kay Stone's concern is with the selection and utilization of images in mass media. Inez Cardozo-Freeman looks at little girls' interpretations of their own adult-role images. Norma McLeod and Marcia Herndon illustrate how an image defines a performer's role. Susan Kalčik's data indicate ways in which contemporary women manipulate popular images of themselves. Roger Abrahams discusses some ways of verbally negotiating and projecting self-images. And Agnes Freudenberg Hostettler demonstrates how the image women hold of themselves and choose to present to others is elaborated in a traditional setting. The first three deal with women's images centrally; the last three have women's images as a peripheral concern, while the McLeod and Herndon paper strikes a middle stance.

Images, as well as the roles consistent with them, are usually thought of as being integrated, static units. In contrast to the formation of stereotypes, the image formation process is one that has received little attention until recently, and none of that work has been in folklore.[44] None, that is, until Stoeltje's paper. She considers the image of frontier woman as a process, a dialectic

---

[43] This issue had its genesis as papers presented at a two-part symposium entitled "Women in Groups: The Organization of Expressive Culture Among Women" at the 1973 annual meeting of the American Folklore Society held in Nashville, Tennessee. Earlier versions of the papers by Inez Cardozo-Freeman, Agnes Freudenberg Hostettler, Susan Kalčik, and Kay Stone were presented at the symposium, as was a much abbreviated version of this essay. The paper by Norma McLeod and Marcia Herndon was first read in much shorter form by Herndon at the 1972 annual meeting of the American Folklore Society held in Austin, Texas.

[44] In addition to Boulding, cited above, see Roger M. Downs and David Stea, eds., *Image and Environment* (Chicago, 1973), and the essays by Spradley, Miller, Galanter, and Pribram, Blumer, Basso, and Zaretsky in James P. Spradley, ed., *Culture and Cognition* (San Francisco, 1972).

between environment and previous cultural attitudes mediated by the new experiences encountered on the frontier. In order to discuss the formation of the images of frontier women (she demonstrates the image to be tri-partite), she finds it necessary to discuss the images of frontier men: both Other and Self are required to define either completely. Her contribution far exceeds the bounds of feminism or regionalism.

The role model of a proper woman as presented in the Grimms' collection of tales is discussed by Stone. She illustrates Disney's further reification of the image to produce the insipid heroine of the many films we can remember from our own childhoods or of those our children see. The comparison between the Grimm-Disney heroine type and kinds of heroines found in other collections is revealing. But rather than stopping with the survey of literature, Stone interviewed women and girls to assess their attitudes toward the role models they had had presented to them in the codified mass-media forms of print and film. Stone's article is one with which most American and Canadian women will readily identify.

In 1973, Cardozo-Freeman did fieldwork among Mexicans and Mexican-Americans. Some of the data she collected during that time form the basis of her article concerning games played by contemporary Mexican girls in the lower socio-economic strata of Mexican society. The implicit and explicit sanctions imposed on the mothers and other adult female kin of the girls are toyed with in the games. Cardozo-Freeman comments on the manifest and latent functions of the games for the girls playing them. She compares the images in the games to the roles of adult Mexican women.

McLeod and Herndon's discussion of the *bormliza*, a Maltese song genre, is an elegant illustration of both the public versus private arena problem and the interrelationship of image and genre. Female *bormliza* singers perform in public, but a woman who performs in public is, by Maltese definition, a prostitute. The paper describes not only the *bormliza* style of singing but also the more socially acceptable singing styles available to Maltese women. The authors discuss as well the Maltese concepts of "public" and "prostitute." The aesthetic system in operation on Malta in regard to singing is complex and is dependent as much upon social factors as it is upon aesthetic ones. Nonetheless, the images of women determine in large measure the genres a particular woman will perform.

Within any community, society, or culture an aesthetic system operates with respect to expressive behavior, and within that aesthetic system are the traditional genres recognized, argued about, and used by folklorists. There are as well what Dan Ben-Amos has characterized as ethnic genres in distinction to analytical categories: "ethnic genres are cultural modes of communication."[45] The traditional genres and the ethnic ones combine to form the system of aesthetics for expressive behavior for any given group.

Usually in Western societies it is the male genres that have been used to define the recognized universe of artistic expression within a group. These recog-

---

[45] Dan Ben-Amos, "Analytical Categories and Ethnic Genres," *Genre*, 2 (1969), 275.

nized, usually male, genres assume the status of "legitimate" folklore genres. Female expressive forms either fit the male mold or they are relegated to a non-legitimate, less-than-expressive category. For instance, we have "tall tales," a male genre of storytelling; the female corollary is exaggeration. Men have "stories" or "yarns"; women "gossip" or "clothesline."[46] Women's expressive vehicles are the nonlegitimate forms, even though they are as ordered and as rule-governed as the male forms. Again Ben-Amos provides a definition when he says that ethnic generic taxonomies "are reflections of the rules for what can be said, in what situation, in what form, by whom and to whom."[47]

It is cumbersome to speak of nonlegitimate genres, but these modes of expression have no common terminology—they are inadmissible as legitimate in the present state of folkloristics. The folklore of women is largely expressed through the use of these nonlegitimate genres.

What are the reasons for the issue of legitimacy in a discussion of men's and women's expressive genres? To say we live in a sexist-ordered world begs the question. At least partial answers are found when the performance settings, the times deemed appropriate for performance, the participants, and the styles of performance and presentation appropriate to each occasion are examined. But a series of emically recognized genres is found in all-female groups. These genres are formed and function in much the way Hannerz described for street-corner men's speech genres. The women's genres have been named (by men?) as "gossip" or "clotheslining"—value-laden and derogatory terms. Though such women's genres are often thought of by women as exchanges of information or memorates germane to a given topic, they may also be read as an expression of verbal artistic creativity or performance.

Regardless of names, the forms *are* recognized by most women. The participants in interactions where the forms are used have a set of expectations as to what is to follow: there is a structured aesthetic operating, to use Prague School terms.[48] Just as Bunzel's Pueblo potters worked with an unconscious form in mind, so too a sense of appropriateness of form exists in women's conversational genres. Discovering these genres, separating them, and learning rules for their generation and transformation may seem a gargantuan task. However, the tools we usually use to analyze known genres can just as easily be used to uncover and discuss new forms, as Kalčik's paper demonstrates.

Kalčik's data were obtained without the permission of the members of the groups in which she recorded; therefore, personal and professional ethics have prohibited her from publishing her data. Others using the model she develops and presents in her article will validate her work. As any woman can testify, the collaborative genre Kalčik describes and analyzes is in operation in coffee klatsches, in supermarkets, in parks where women gather while watching their children, and in many other similar situations. Women commonly use other collaborative genres as well—genres in which the performer role is passed

---

[46] I am indebted to Roger D. Abrahams for calling this term to my attention.

[47] Ben-Amos, 285.

[48] See especially Jan Mukarovsky, "The Esthetics of Language," in *A Prague School Reader on Esthetics, Literary Structure, and Style*, ed. Paul L. Garvin (Washington, D.C., 1964), 31–69.

from one group member to another, often in what appears to be the middle of an utterance. I look forward to more studies like Kalčik's, which will further illuminate these genres and, it is hoped, firmly attach a sense of validity to their study.

Abrahams also discusses an unnamed, nonlegitimate, ethnic genre in his paper on black women's speech styles. He approaches his material from a sociological perspective, thus providing another dimension that will aid in the eventual legitimization of women's speech behavior. He notes, as does Kalčik, that women's speech styles are ordered and formulaic, allowing participants, or those present, to anticipate the form and partial content of what is to follow. In contrast to similar styles among men, the women's speech behavior requires the participation of others. The performer role is a floating one. The women collaborate and support each other's presentation, though they may not agree with the content of that presentation.

Despite my present emphasis, it must not be assumed that all women's genres are verbal ones. Within women's expected role-behavior, some things are segregated out for elaboration, are foregrounded, and achieve the status of vehicles for artistic expression. Because an item has instrumental utility, it need not necessarily be excluded from artistic or expressive slots. Thus, women's traditional clothing is a vehicle for expressive behavior and is the subject of Hostettler's paper. She illustrates how the articulation of politics, economics, history, and folklore have combined to revitalize and elaborate on what had been a dying tradition. We have accepted as fact the notion that tourism slaughters and commercializes traditional arts and crafts; Hostettler demonstrates that this notion is not valid.

Firestone wrote, "Just as male audiences have always demanded, and received, male art to reinforce their particular view of reality, so a female audience demands a 'female' art to reinforce the female reality."[49] She was sounding a call for this art to arise and be developed. But women have already been defined and have defined themselves. The images already exist and are manipulated strategically as well as artistically by women, often in ethnic genres. The articles that follow will convince even the most skeptical that the art is not only alive and well but also that it has a history as well as a future.[50]

---

[49] Firestone, 167.

[50] I would like to express my appreciation for the encouragement and help which Roger Abrahams and Richard Bauman so graciously gave me in helping me to set up the 1973 American Folklore Society symposium. Also, I want to acknowledge the kind assistance of Susan Kalčik, Elizabeth Warnock Fernea, Beverly J. Stoeltje, and James Malarkey.

Women and Folklore

"... like Ann's gynecologist or the time I was almost raped"

Personal Narratives in Women's Rap Groups

SUSAN KALČIK

IN CLAIRE FARRER'S INTRODUCTION TO THIS ISSUE, she notes the need for studies of women's collaborative folklore. One source of such folklore is the women's "rap group" narrative. Consciousness-raising rap groups, developed by the Women's Movement as a first step toward liberation, are composed of small numbers of women who meet to share their experiences and, ideally, in the process discover that their problems are often social and are related to the larger problem of the oppression of women. I shall discuss various strategies of interaction characteristic of rap groups and the structure of a type of personal narrative I call the kernel story, which reflects these strategies and in some ways is constructed by them. A brief examination of other studies of the relationship between narration and context helps focus on particular aspects of the rap-group narratives as emergent structures. No definitive statement about women's storytelling, interaction, or use of language is attempted except in terms of the rap-group situation and narratives analyzed here, but important questions and considerations are raised that can be applied to further research in these three areas.

The material on which this article is based was collected during my involvement with two Women's Liberation groups. In the first, located at a midwestern university, I acted as codirector. Consciousness-raising was but one of the activities of the women. Participants in the rap sessions, which met once a week during the school year, were chiefly white women faculty and students, and, though membership changed frequently, a core membership usually attended. Most sessions were directed by discussion leaders and a topic or an outline to follow was suggested. The second group, in which I participated as a member only, was formed in a southwestern university community. It was a small, stable group of white students and working women who met once a week for three months. The group had no formal leadership and no stated goals or discussion guidelines. In addition to participation in these two groups I have also observed and collected data in various one-shot women's functions such as workshops, NOW conventions, and women's career days. Personal narratives that occur in all such groups of women are sex specific and context specific. Their selection by narrators and to some extent their telling and structure are affected by the shared goal, not always stated, of trying in some manner to cope with women's oppression.

The four most common characters in these personal narratives, besides the women themselves, are (1) men in general and husbands, lovers, boyfriends, and male friends in particular; (2) other women; (3) mothers; and (4) male doctors. Mothers, for example, were generally discussed in terms of what they believed or told their daughters about other women, sex, and menstruation; a typical statement is, "When I had my first period, my mother told me I would have to stop jumping rope, so for a long time I thought if I wasn't careful, my stomach would fall out somehow."

A major subject of the stories is oppression experiences women have in jobs (low salary, slow promotion, humiliations), in school (treatment by male professors and students, advice from counselors), and in situations relating to dating, marriage, and living together. Another frequent theme is self-discovery, which often involves exchanging information about physiology, a subject on which many women are ill informed. I have heard a number of personal narratives about vaginal infections and how doctors do or do not treat them, for example. Rape (attempted, unreported, or of men by women) and names (their significance, changing and keeping them, their relation to a woman's identity) were subjects that also received much attention.

The importance of these characters and themes to women interested in liberation is suggested by the fact that many of them appear in published Women's Liberation literature, which includes, among others, articles and books on men's role in oppression; mothers' effects on their daughters; rape, the crime in which the victim is treated as the criminal; women's bodies and illnesses; and the relationship between women and doctors. Also significant in Women's Liberation literature are the many studies of language and women's use of it. In the consciousness-raising group, women often for the first time explore their ability to manipulate language in a respectful climate. The rap group is talking, talking to bring women together. Therefore the stories told there are important not only in terms of their content but also in terms of what they tell us about how women talk and how they tell stories.

My study of women's rap groups reveals certain significant strategies that the women applied to all group interactions, including the telling of personal narratives. The first of these involves politeness rules and breaches thereof. The women seemed to value decorum highly; they asked permission to speak (one way of getting into a story) and tried to make sure that others were completely finished before another woman began. There may be some difference at this point between the male and female codes, men tending, in women's views, to be less polite. A woman once told me that she never got to speak in a seminar because she kept waiting to make sure the male students were finished talking; they never were. The women in the rap group took pains to see that everyone spoke, often asking for the response or comments of someone who had not spoken much, and they disliked any one person dominating the meeting. Many women began and ended with apologies: for speaking, for the content of their speech, for speaking too long. In other words, the women consistently and elaborately filled the apology slot. However, one politeness rule of speech interaction was commonly disregarded with impunity. The "you talk–I listen, I talk–you listen" rule was broken often, and only rarely did its breach appear to offend. Interruptions in the form of questions or comments might be made throughout another woman's talk or story, often before she had ended her first sentence. An example is this opening of a story about how men do not let women assert themselves and how women are afraid to do so.

Narrator: "Speaking of asserting oneself, my guy and I were talking about this and he wanted me to. . . ."
Woman: "Oh, he . . . ? That's cool." (Implied is the feeling that it is remarkable a male would want the woman to act assertively.)

The second strategy involves a pair of contrasting patterns of interaction: competition and support. Either or both of these might stimulate a series or chain of stories told by different narrators. Story chaining could result from a competitive desire to "top" the previous narrator's story or from an urge to support her by sharing a similar experience. However, the women as a group seemed to value the latter and resented signs of competitiveness. Competition occurred most often in large groups or when many of the women did not know each other. Support for other women is a goal of rap groups, and this ideal was reached more consistently in small, intimate groups. Support was expressed linguistically (comments during and after another woman's story, questions asked to show interest, and stories told by others to show how similar their experiences were) and paralinguistically, in the form of sympathetic noises, facial expressions, and gestures. The women almost never gossiped about members who were not there, avoided direct criticism of each other, and tried to keep others from criticizing themselves.

Humor, a third strategy, was used supportively to keep the group close and to underline the feeling of "we're all in this together." Much of this, however, the women accomplished by turning the humor in on themselves rather than on supposed oppressors. Humor might be used to support a woman, to help ease tension when a story or discussion got too heavy: "Well dear, put on some makeup and you'll feel better." This is an example of humor achieved by applying a stereotype to the woman herself, as is the following apology made by a woman who was having some difficulty expressing herself: "Well, you know how we women are; our hormones get up in our brains and fuck up our thinking." Even jokes about oppressors took this form; the same sort of clichés were put into their mouths: "My doctor thinks my vaginal infection is all in my head; he has a strange picture of my anatomy." This superficially self-denigrating humor, by stressing the stereotypes and problems the women shared, worked to strengthen the group.

Three other common strategies involving speech specifically are filling in, tying together, and serializing. Much of the women's speech had an unfinished or undeveloped quality; they tended to talk in phrases or sentences that trailed off, especially those who had little experience with being listened to by a group. It was not necessary, in fact, to be explicit when an experience was shared by everyone, for a few words were enough to trace the outline of a story. Gaps were filled in individually and internally or out loud by questions, answers, and comments when the group wanted or needed a fuller picture.

New points of discussion and new stories were usually preceded by some attempt to tie them into the discussion. The opening of a story was often an explanation of how it tied in with the last one told or with a story told earlier or even at another session, and group members other than the narrator made such comments on how a woman's story fit with someone else's. This desire for a sense of continuity was also revealed in the serializing of stories. Often a series of stories involving one of the women grew over several meetings, either because the narrator volunteered the latest installment of a story told earlier or because someone, motivated by politeness or a desire to support, questioned her about recent developments.

Some of the above strategies, especially those that involve interrupting, making supportive comments, asking questions, making humorous interjections, and filling in, resulted occasionally in the group production of a story. A careful study of the transcripts of some personal narratives from the rap-group sessions shows that a story begun by one woman might be developed and even refocused by the questions and comments of the group members and the answers and comments of the narrator.

The success of these strategies in bringing women closer together and leading them to a greater awareness of their common bonds and problems is demonstrated by the fact that many of the strategies are in Women's Liberation literature on rules or suggestions for conducting consciousness-raising sessions. But they are significant on another level in that in terms of women's speech and interaction they seem to be an expression of an underlying aesthetic or organizing principle: harmony.

This review of the common characters, themes, and strategies I found in rap-group interaction and storytelling provides an introduction to my main point, which concerns the structure of one kind of story that appeared in the sessions. When I began working with the material from rap groups, two recurring problems suggested the necessity of looking at the structure of some women's stories in a new way. One difficulty was in naming what I called "stories" or "personal narratives." Some persons to whom I showed my data did not think they fit into these categories. Many women as well as men would not see that there are two stories in my title. William Labov and Joshua Waletzsky's study "Narrative Analysis"[1] was of no help in choosing the proper label because they had collected their narratives from males; there is no comparable work on women's

---

[1] "Narrative Analysis: Oral Versions of Personal Experience," American Ethnological Society Proceedings (Spring, 1966), 12–44.

narrative. I eventually decided to stick with the terms *story* or *personal narrative* because that was what I and most of the women to whom I showed my data called them, and we were, in this case, the folk. The second problem I encountered involved the folk belief that women cannot tell stories or jokes correctly, a belief often expressed by women and men. Some women do tend to tell the punch line or the most important part first, instead of leading up to it; this is exactly how the stories I am discussing are told. The two problems, which suggest that women cannot tell stories and that what women do tell are not real stories, lead me to conclude that some women's stories are not structured in ways that have been commonly studied. One such narrative type recurrent in my rap-group material I call the *kernel story*.

Most often a kernel story is a brief reference to the subject, the central action, or an important piece of dialogue from a longer story. In this form one might say it is a kind of potential story, especially if the details are not known to the audience. It might be clearer to call this brief reference the *kernel* and what develops from it the *kernel story*, keeping in mind, however, that many of these kernels do not develop beyond the first stage into kernel stories. Kernel stories lack a specific length, structure, climax, or point, although a woman familiar with the genre or subject may predict fairly accurately where a particular story will go. The story developed from the kernel can take on a different size and shape depending on the context in which it is told.

The structure of a kernel story, therefore, is fluid. It may be very brief, consisting of an introduction of some sort and the kernel itself. The story may not be developed beyond this kernel if the audience already knows the story and an allusion to it is considered sufficient or if the kernel is offered by way of a supportive comment, indicating that the narrator has had a similar experience to one being presented by someone who has the floor. A kernel may not be developed if no one expresses an interest or asks any questions, if the narrator does not choose to tell any more, or if another narrator wins a competition to speak next. If the narrator does want to tell more of her story, however, or to answer questions about it, she may expand the kernel by means of several devices. Kernel stories may be developed by adding exposition and detail or by adding nonnarrative elements such as a rationale for telling the story; an apology; an analysis of the characters, events, or theme; or an emotional response to the story. A story also can be developed by stringing several kernels together to produce an elaborate story or a unit longer than a story, such as a serial. In addition, most of these stories, even in the briefest form, have some introduction or opening remark, most often one tying them to earlier stories or discussion. Common are "that reminds me . . ." "speaking of . . ." and the single word "like" as I have used it in my title, " '. . . like Ann's gynecologist or the time I was almost raped.' "

Jeanne Watson and Robert J. Potter's notion of conversational resource may shed some light on the fluidity of the kernel story's structure.[2] They point out that the nominal topic of a conversation is a resource the group may draw upon

---

[2] "An Analytic Unit for the Study of Interaction," *Human Relations*, 15 (1962), 245–263.

in various ways and, hence, "sociable interaction consists of the elaboration of conversational resource."[3] Different ways of developing the resource once it has been introduced depend on what it is, the participants' relations to it, and their experience and expectations of interaction. Individual experience or collective stereotypes will affect the process of association each group member has with the resource, be that association conscious or unconscious, logical or emotional, literal or symbolic. To keep interaction going, members will choose the associations most meaningful to the group, that is, the ones that will evoke response or enable others to join in.[4] In a conversation then, "movement can be viewed as departure from the point of origin in some direction(s) which the participants find meaningful; or, alternatively, as a kind of spiraling activity, in which participants move away from the resource and back again, with each 'circle' shedding new light upon the resource, utilizing new facets of it, and perhaps adding to the collective product something of the personal quality of the speaker(s)."[5]

In the women's talk I have been describing the notion of resource can be viewed as working in two ways. First, a topic of conversation, such as rape or women's guilt, can be seen as a conversational resource in Watson and Potter's terms and the telling of personal narratives and references to narratives, or categories of narratives, evoked by the subject can be seen as methods for exploiting that resource. Second, a personal narrative itself may be a conversational resource, which the group adds to, shapes, and even changes. This accounts partly for the changing or fluid structure of the kernel story I have described.

Two processes defined by Watson and Potter (association, developing the resource to serve the momentary and long-range needs of the group) are central in rap-group talk and storytelling. The exploitation of the resources and contextual variables of a rap group guide the emergence of certain stories and types of stories.

In other words, kernel stories are emergent structures. They emerge from the context in which they appear to support another woman's story, to help achieve a tone of harmony in the group, or to fit the topic under discussion or develop that topic with related ideas. Thus, the climax or point of the story can shift from telling to telling; different parts of the story, events or details, can be foregrounded to make the story suit the point the narrator wishes to make. Nonnarrative elements are important because they can easily be used to shape the story to fit the situation. It is important to note that this shifting can be done both by the narrator when she chooses what of the story she will tell this time and by the group members when they ask questions or reveal in comments what they think the point of the story is or ought to be.

The kernel story, then, is a conversational genre of folklore in two ways. First, conversation can become part of the story, and, second, it is structured in part by the conversational context from which it emerges.

---

[3] Ibid., 251.
[4] Ibid., 252.
[5] Ibid.

Kernel stories form part of the repertoires of the individual women but, when known to the others, they can become part of the group's repertoire as well. Other women will refer to them and even tell them.

An example of the kernel story is one that was very popular in the first group to which I belonged. Originally it was told by a faculty member about one of her students. The student, talking to her professor after class, seemed very disturbed about the grade she had received on a literature exam, and the professor was confused at first, since the grade was an A. Finally the student explained that she had hoped to do poorly on the exam because her boyfriend had threatened to take back his fraternity pin if she continued to get a higher grade-point average than he did. This story might be told, and often was, in discussions about how men do not like women to display their intelligence. But it might just as easily be told by the narrator, choosing details and a tone unsympathetic with the heroine, to argue that women are stupid to deny their abilities. Or this latter interpretation might be pointed out by a member of the group who is responding to the story as told in the first case, and the meaning of the story might then shift to this new thesis by way of group commentary. As the meaning shifts, the narrator could add details that support the new thesis, such as the fact that the girl had read only half the assigned material in the hope that this would hobble her enough to keep her from making above a C, or the fact that the boyfriend was simultaneously dating another girl just in case the first did not lower her average. When this story became familiar to many of the group's members, it was often alluded to in kernel form to support another story with a similar theme; someone would say, "Right, like X's student."

Several other studies of the relationship between the structure of the text and the structure of the context in folkloric narrative are useful in examining that relationship in the emergent structures of kernel stories. Regna Darnell, in her study of a Cree narrative performance, describes a gradual transition backward from present through past Indian life to the mythologic time of the tale as a process the storyteller must go through before telling his narrative; after the narrative is told, the order is reversed.[6] The particular performance she describes involves a tale with two endings. The first ending is the formal one; the second, providing "a gradual transition back to the everyday conversational world,"[7] served as a moral or epilogue addressed to the particular audience. By capitalizing on the fact that one member of his audience wore a beard and by weaving the detail of beards into this second ending, the Cree performer could draw his audience into the tale-telling situation; thus he expressed an acceptance of and closeness to them.[8] The storytelling context, then, affected the content of his tale as it did in the women's kernel stories. It is important to note, however, that in the Cree example the structure of the situation, the structure of the narrative, and the relationship between performer and audience

[6] "Generational Differences in Cree Narrative Performance," in Explorations in the Ethnography of Speaking, ed. Richard Bauman and Joel Sherzer (Cambridge, 1974), 315–336.
[7] Ibid., 335.
[8] Ibid.

are more formal and fixed than in the rap groups, and the freedom to draw on contextual resources more inhibited.

A comparison of rap-group narratives with Kirshenblatt-Gimblett's study of the use of parable in conversation reveals a similar point. In her paper, Kirshenblatt-Gimblett argues that the effectiveness of a particular proverb stems from the way its structure maps onto the structure of the situation in which it is told.[9] "The *social* interaction within the parable itself is a corrective ritual" that closely parallels the interaction of the real-life situation in which it is told in order to relieve the tension of family members involved in a corrective ritual that has reached an impasse.[10] In the rap groups, too, narrative structure tended to parallel interactional structure; for example, each is supportive in character. However, the parable is a relatively set form, even more so than the Cree tale. In effect rap-group members had an advantage over the parable teller because, rather than selecting a story structure parallel to the situation, they could select a kernel story and change its structure to meet contextual needs. Moreover, the parable is applied to a past situation, however recent that past may be, a situation with an identifiable structure. In the rap groups this could not always happen because often both the structure of the story and the situation were emerging simultaneously and interacting with each other.

It seems then that folklore performance situations differ significantly in the possibilities for the presence and use of emergent forms. In Harvey Sacks's examination of joke telling (again, jokes are a less flexible form of narrative than kernel stories) in a conversational situation, he identifies three main divisions of the storytelling process: a preface sequence, a telling sequence, and a response sequence. He points out that in each stage the performer and audience have various options or choices. For example, an intended teller may make an initial statement in the preface sequence, including some or all of these components: "an offer to tell or a request for a chance to tell the joke or story; an initial characterization of it; some reference to the time of the story events' occurrence or of the joke's reception; and, for jokes particularly, a reference to from whom it was received if its prior teller is known or known of by recipients." When the offer to tell a story is made, the audience has a range of possible response choices, including the expression of a desire to listen or not to listen.[11]

In effect, such options provide a minimal structure or framework for interaction and performance in more formal situations like the Cree storytelling and in the less formal context of conversation. It is from the interaction of contextual variables such as topic or resource within the minimal framework that the structure of a particular narrative and narrative event emerges. In the rap group the general goals of the sessions, women's rules of speech and interaction, the women's past experiences with each other, and the limited range of subjects discussed constitute a framework from the particulars of which the group's interaction and stories emerge.

---

9 "A Parable in Context: A Social Interactional Analysis of Storytelling Performance," to appear in *Folklore and Communication*, ed. Dan Ben-Amos and Kenneth S. Goldstein, 4, 14–17, 21–30.

10 Ibid., 21.

11 "An Analysis of the Course of a Joke's Telling in Conversation" in *Ethnography of Speaking.*

Further investigation may show that the kernel story as described in this paper is uniquely a woman's genre. One might conjecture that the structure of such stories parallels the rhythm of many women's lives, filled as they are with small tasks and constant interruptions from children, husbands, telephones, repairmen. It is common in our culture that men and women do not value women's speech or stories; they are labeled "just gossip" or, significantly, "women's talk." That women have thus learned to be brief and apologetic in their speech unless encouraged seems to be reflected in the story structure I have described. The fact that the stories I found were a group product may have its roots in women's sense of powerlessness and their realization that they need to work together.

This study of women's collaborative lore suggests other areas of investigation. For example, how are these stories from women's rap groups related to women's folklore in general and especially to women's storytelling? And what can they, along with other types of women's stories, tell us about women's culture, world view, and speech? For example, the number of rape stories may reveal a sense of powerlessness and vulnerability on the part of women. A study of personal narrative and storytelling is certainly one way to approach and define a women's aesthetic. And the study of women's storytelling will further the study of conversational genres of folklore in general if in no other way than the important one of balancing a one-sided view of storytelling that results from collecting data chiefly from one half of the members of a society.

Games Mexican Girls Play*

INEZ CARDOZO-FREEMAN

"MY GRANDMOTHER TOLD ME TO GUARD MYSELF FROM MEN for they are a danger. I don't protect myself from work. The thing I'm afraid of is men."[1] This quotation is an expression of the attitudes of many women in the Mexican folk culture.[2] Why do so many women of this culture hold this view with respect to men? How do Mexican women view their life situation? And, finally, do the games they play as children express and reflect these views?

Between March and November of 1973, I collected games and songs and interviewed thirty-seven women in Mexico between the ages of fifteen and sixty-three and seventeen women between the ages of twenty-two and fifty-nine born in Mexico but now living in the United States. For evidence in this study I am using both these collected materials and studies done by other scholars to demonstrate that some of the games Mexican women play as young girls and recall vividly as adults reflect their views of themselves and their life situation and that this situation reflects an adult life that is distressing—a life of invasion, betrayal, abandonment, and forced seclusion.

Although I rather strongly state that, in general, the position of women in the Mexican folk culture leaves much to be desired, it would be unjust to give the impression that all women share the experiences and attitudes expressed here. Nor do I wish to suggest that all Mexican men regard women as being something less than human; this is simply not true. I offer evidence of a situation that existed very commonly in the Mexican folk culture in the past and still exists now, though to a lesser degree; this situation is reflected in some of the games Mexican girls play. Of course, Mexico is undergoing great changes, using the United States as a model, and these changes are affecting every aspect of Mexican culture, including the position of women in the folk culture.

Men regard women in a very distinct and particular way in Mexico. Arnulfo

---

* The research, study, and preparation of the material in this article were made possible by a fellowship granted in 1973 by the National Endowment for the Humanities.

[1] Oscar Lewis, *Life in a Mexican Village* (Urbana, Illinois, 1963), 362.

[2] "Folk culture" refers here to the Mexican peasant class.

Castillo, a former migrant farm worker born in Mexico and now living in Ohio, states: "In Mexico the man orders and the woman obeys. It is a custom or inheritance that has lived from generation to generation." In the words of the great Mexican poet Octavio Paz: "The Spanish attitude toward women is very simple. It is expressed quite brutally and concisely in these two sayings: 'A woman's place is in the home with a broken leg,' and 'Between a female saint and a male saint a wall of mortared stone.' Woman is a domesticated wild animal, lecherous and sinful from birth, who must be subdued with a stick and guided by the 'reins of religion.' "[3] Although he is speaking of the "Spanish" attitude, the same point of view may be applied to Mexico, which has inherited so much of Spanish culture and thought.

Women in the Mexican folk culture are expected to be submissive, docile, self-sacrificing, and uncomplainingly stoic in their acceptance of all the many restrictions placed on them.[4] For example, from puberty a woman is confined to the home. Anywhere she goes she must be accompanied by others.[5] When she marries, again she is discouraged from leaving the house unaccompanied and from having other women companions; only women in the immediate family are allowed into her circle.[6] This restriction is maintained to protect the honor of the husband.

A Mexican woman is discouraged from expressing her feelings about her situation; there is an emphasis on formality not only with respect to negative feelings but positive ones as well.[7] A woman is taught that she must submit to all that happens to her without complaint. She is taught that her rights belong to her husband; in a sense, she has no rights.[8]

A woman does not always look upon sex as pleasurable. Rather she generally regards sex at first with fear, then later with distaste, as an obligation that must be endured.[9] Often in my interviews women referred to sex as *el abuso del hombre*, "the abuse of the man."[10] Research points out that Mexican men often do not want their wives to enjoy sex; "indeed a wife's enjoyment is often considered by a husband as a justifiable cause for suspicion of infidelity."[11]

Finally, having babies is not the great pleasure of Mexican women, as is so often erroneously believed.[12] Rather it is often the men who want many children and not the women. Lewis' research indicates this,[13] and my talks with many women also confirm this observation. Women sometimes view pregnancy as a punishment from God and childbearing as something that must be stoically endured.[14] Almost all the women I talked to referred to pregnancy as an illness

---

[3] *The Labyrinth of Solitude*, trans. Lysander Kemp (New York, 1961), 36.
[4] Ari Kiev, *Curanderismo: Mexican American Folk Psychiatry* (New York, 1968), 59.
[5] Lewis, 395.
[6] Ibid., 327.
[7] Kiev, 60–61.
[8] Ibid., 62.
[9] Ibid., 59.
[10] See also Lewis, 362.
[11] Kiev, 59.
[12] See also Lewis, 353.
[13] Ibid., 320.
[14] Ibid., 353.

and called the experience "being *sick* with child."[15] On the other hand, the men I talked to openly expressed a desire for many children.[16] I was told by some women that having many children insures that a man will not be betrayed by his wife.[17] Indeed, a pregnant wife with many little ones clinging to her is not likely to be having liaisons with lovers.

Of all the impressions I received while in Mexico, one stands out sharply from all the rest. Everywhere I went, whether to the market places in the provinces or the elegant Zona Rosa of Mexico City, I saw the same scene: a very, very young woman, at the most seventeen, holding by the hand a child who looked to be no older than two. In her arms she carried a tiny baby tightly wrapped in a *rebozo*, and always her belly was big with child. Often these child-mothers wore no shoes, and I was constantly reminded of a saying so common in certain areas of the United States: "Keep them barefoot and pregnant."

I spoke to many women about their situation, and always their sadness disturbed me. They were not joyful in their motherhood, they were resigned. Several of the women had been abandoned by their husbands. Santiago Ramírez, in his study *El mexicano: psicología de sus motivaciones*, makes some intriguing comments with respect to this abandonment of the wife-mother. He states that when a child is born his mother wraps him in a *rebozo* and holds him closely and securely to her in a kind of womblike paradise. But the moment the next child arrives the mother suddenly dumps him out of the *rebozo*, replacing him with the new child; he suddenly is thrown from paradise, and he never forgets this betrayal. Ramírez' research shows that in seventy percent of all cases abandonment coincided with pregnancy of the wife.[18]

Women of the folk culture believe a long period without sex is necessary when a woman gives birth to a child. A woman will tell you a year, even two years is best for this "rest" from *el abuso del hombre*.[19] They are seeking, of course, to avoid pregnancy, which happens with such exhausting frequency, but their husbands seldom cooperate, as the evidence so clearly shows.[20] To some Mexican men, having many children is proof of manhood.

Machismo, in its most positive aspects, is attractive and admirable. Basically it means "being a man," being honorable, dignified, and courageous, protecting one's good name. *Machismo* at its worst, however, borders almost on pathology and exaggerates and distorts beyond recognition the qualities described above. Professor Ernesto Scheffler, La escuela de filosofía y letres, Universitaria de Guanajuato, Gto., México, described this aspect of *machismo* to me as "patriarchy at its maximum level of degeneracy."[21] Octavio Paz states that the *macho* represents the Mexican version of the masculine pole of life. "One word sums

---

[15] Ibid., 354.
[16] Ibid.
[17] Ibid., 328.
[18] Monografías psicoanalíticas, I (Mexico City, 1972), 88–91.
[19] Lewis, 362.
[20] Ibid., 326.
[21] See also Américo Paredes, "The United States, Mexico, and Machismo," *Journal of the Folklore Institute*, I (1971), 18.

up the aggressiveness, insensitivity, invulnerability, and other attributes of the *macho*: that word is power."[22] This exaggerated concept of manliness juxtaposed with the concept of the "ideal" Mexican woman, who must be submissive, docile, long-suffering, brings into focus two polarities that feed off each other with unpleasant consequences.

Women in Mexico live in a restrictive, male-dominated culture and therefore resent and fear men. Everything that keeps a woman suppressed is bound up in values that are determined by men. These restrictive values thwart personal expression and growth. Not being allowed to express feelings of anger, frustration, and hostility, the woman develops pronounced attitudes of self-righteousness and martyrdom, which result in conscious and unconscious divisiveness within the family with the mother often playing a harmful role in regard to her children.[23] The mother is always reminding her children of how much she has suffered for them and how therefore the children owe everything to their mother. Women also project the hostility they feel toward their husbands onto their children.[24] Thus girls grow up fearing men, regarding them as the cause of their mother's plight, and assuming that their role will be similar to that which their mother endures.[25]

From the age of nine or ten a young girl in the Mexican folk culture is beginning to assume the duties of a woman, caring for younger brothers and sisters, preparing meals, and so on.[26] She must set aside play very early in life. Even before she marries, therefore, she is "chained to her hearth."[27] She marries early, around the age of fifteen, even earlier in years past. Very often she scarcely knows the man she marries; certainly she has never been allowed to be alone with him prior to the marriage, and custom precludes preparing her for her first sexual experience.[28]

If a woman dares to show she is an individual, dares to be independent or aggressive, or manifests a liking for sex, the Mexican folk culture is so shocked it assumes she is *embrujada*, "bewitched," or *loca*, "crazy," and will seek out a *curandero*, a folk doctor or folk psychiatrist, as Ari Kiev calls the *curandero*.[29] Women who are not submissive and docile are so foreign to the culture that they are regarded as abnormal.

Folklore can serve as a safe vehicle for protest against such harsh restrictions and attitudes imposed by a society. Some of the games Mexican girls play may give expression to the feelings of hostility, fear, and frustration that the Mexican woman endures in her culture. She is not allowed to rebel or change her situation, but as a young girl she can play out her life as she imagines it will be when she reaches womanhood. In a sense, her play as a young girl appears

[22] Paz, 81.
[23] See also Kiev, 55.
[24] Ibid.
[25] Ibid., 59.
[26] Lewis, 389.
[27] Arnulfo Castillo, personal communication.
[28] Lewis, 326.
[29] Kiev, 58.

to be practice or preparation for the pain and injustice she must endure as a woman.

Her games are sometimes frightening, others are funny, still others are poignantly sad. Many can be found in all other Spanish-speaking countries, as well as in Portugal, and we can assume that many of the attitudes expressed in the games are held to some degree in all Spanish and Portuguese cultures. The peculiar male dominance so exaggerated in Mexican culture exists also in Spain and Portugal and their colonies, particularly with respect to the seclusion and confinement of women within the home; this is not a phenomenon exclusive to Mexico. Much of the restrictiveness can be traced in part to a cultural lag,[30] to eight hundred years of Moorish influence in the Iberian Peninsula,[31] and to the Spanish and Portuguese Catholic influence, which helps promulgate the idea that women are evil and dangerous and in need of tight controls and supervision.

One game, a *rondo*, or circle game, is an obvious metaphor for sex by force, or rape. Most intriguing is that this song-game is by far the most popular game played by young girls in Mexico. I collected it everywhere I went. Always it was the first game women gave me. Initially it seems simply a lovely song and game, yet if one looks very carefully one sees that the language, the actions, and the description of how the game is played are filled with sexual metaphor, but, most importantly, it is a metaphor of force and violence that colors all of what is happening.

The game is called "Doña Blanca," or "María Blanca," and according to Vicente T. Mendoza it originated in Spain. Although I collected many versions, for my purposes here I use Mendoza's because he gives a written description of how the game is played.[32] Notice the imagery of violence in the language and actions. Notice the attitude of María Blanca toward the *jicotillo*, who represents the male.[33] Notice also the attitudes of the other girls toward the *jicotillo* and toward María Blanca; they resent the *jicotillo* and are protective of her. *Blanca* is the Spanish word for "white" and suggests, of course, a virgin. The circle seems a sexual symbol for the female.

María Blanca

Todos: María Blanca está cubierta
          con pilares de oro y plata.

---

[30] I am endebted to Américo Paredes for pointing this out to me.

[31] Apparently Moorish attitudes toward women have not changed: "To the average Moslem, a woman is a mere accessory to life. . . . She is bred solely to produce children, preferably male, and in rural areas to help with labor. When not in use she is relegated to *purdah*, the nun-like existence she must lead shut off from contact with all but her closest family. Her thoughts, so far as she is allowed any, are given to her by her husband." Fergus M. Bordewich, "Where Women Are an Annoyance That Disturbs the Symmetry of Life," *The New York Times*, December 9, 1973, Section 10, p. 1.

[32] *Lírica infantil de México* (Mexico City, 1951), 90–91.

[33] The name *jicote* refers to a stinging insect of Mexico. In the village of Cholula, *lobocito* (*lobo* means "wolf") is substituted for *jicotillo*.

> Jicotillo: Romperemos un pilar
> para ver la María Blanca.
>
> Todos: ¿Quién es ese jicotillo
> que anda en pos de María Blanca?
>
> Jicotillo: Yo soy ese, yo soy ese
> que anda en pos de María Blanca.

A continuación se desarrolla el diálogo siguiente; mientras, la niña que hace de María Blanca está en medio del círculo, fingiendo que hace oración, de rodillas:

> Jicotillo: ¿Dónde está María Blanca?
>
> Todos: Está haciendo oración.
>
> Jicotillo: ¿Para quién?
>
> Todos: Para Dios.
>
> Jicotillo: ¿Y para mí?
>
> Todos: Para usted un cuerno bien retorcido.

Entonces el jicotillo trata de romper el círculo, forzando las manos en distintos lugares, y empujando hacia adentro, pregunta:

> Jicotillo: ¿De qué es este pilar?
>
> Todos: De oro.
>
> Jicotillo: ¿Y éste?
>
> Todos: De plata.

Y así sucesivamente le contestan que de mármol, de hiero, de plomo, de yeso, de ladrillo, de cera y de popote; entonces se rompe el círculo y penetra en él, mientras María Blanca huye protegida por los demás, que le cierran el paso al jicotillo. Cuando logra alcanzar a María Blanca dice:

> Jicotillo: Póngase al lado del sol.

A la siguiente niña, que hizo de María Blanca, le dice:

> María Blanca: Póngase del lado de la sombra.

Y así sucesivamente hasta que quedan muy pocas niñas en el círculo.

[Girls: María Blanca is covered with pillars of gold and silver. *Jicotillo*: Let us force apart (or tear) a pillar to see María Blanca. Girls: Who is this *jicotillo* who comes in pursuit of María Blanca? *Jicotillo*: I am this *jicotillo* who comes in pursuit of María Blanca. (A continuation of the dialogue develops as follows; meanwhile, the girl who is María Blanca is in the middle of the circle on her knees, pretending she is praying.) *Jicotillo*: Where is María Blanca? Girls: She is saying her prayers. *Jicotillo*: For whom? Girls: For God. *Jicotillo*: And for me? Girls: For you a well-twisted horn.[34] (Then the *jicotillo* tries to tear open the circle, forcing with his hands in distinct places, and pressing forward to get inside, he asks:) *Jicotillo*: What is this pillar made of? Girls: Of gold. *Jicotillo*: And this one? Girls: Of silver. And in this way they continue answering: Of marble, of iron, of lead, of plaster, of brick, of wax, of straw. (Then

[34] This might be interpreted as a possible betrayal of the male by the female or as a metaphor for rejection of penile intrusion.

he breaks the circle and penetrates inside of it, while María Blanca flees, protected by the others who close the passage of the *jicotillo*. When he succeeds in overtaking María Blanca, he says:) *Jicotillo*: Place yourself in the sun. (And the next girl, who becomes María Blanca, says:) María Blanca: Place yourself in the darkness, or shadows. (In this way they continue until very few girls are left forming the circle.)]

To me this game is a subconscious expression of fear of the male and of sex and is a desire on the part of the female to protect herself, or to wall herself off from male intrusion or penetration.[35] The sad ending, both in life and in the game, is that the *jicotillo*, or male, always succeeds in penetrating or breaking through because his persistence, his aggressiveness, eventually brings about a collapse of the pillars; against force the girls must spread apart to let the *jicotillo* in. Finally, when the *jicotillo* has destroyed the pillars he demands that María Blanca "place herself in the sun," or be happy, and she replies, "Place yourself in the shadows," or be sad. This game symbolically portrays the invasion of the woman that is the beginning of all her misery. The loss of her virginity (the destruction of the pillars) opens the way to her unhappy adult experience. When Mexican girls play this game they enact symbolically, whether they are aware of it or not, what they view their lives to be—an invasion and violation of their bodies, their spirits, and their personalities.

The next game sings of betrayal and abandonment. It also is a lovely *rondo* and very popular today. It is called *"Naranja dulce,"* or Sweet Orange. One girl, who represents the soldier-lover, stands inside the circle. Sometimes a boy takes this part, as in all games here that call for a male figure. When the girls sing, the one in the circle who plays the part of the male enacts what they are singing. He chooses a girl, then asks for an embrace. She in turn wonders whether he will keep his promise to her; the notes of war sound, she cries, he says good-bye, he calls her *señora* instead of *señorita*, implying she is not a virgin.

Naranja dulce

Naranja dulce, limón partido,
Dame un abrazo que yo te pido.

Si fueron falsos tus juramentos
En otros tiempos se olvidarán.

Toca la marcha, mi pecho llora,
Adiós, señora, yo ya me voy.[36]

[Sweet orange, sliced lemon, give me an embrace I beg you. If your promises are false, in other times they will be forgotten. The march plays. My heart cries. Good-bye, madam, I leave you now.]

---

[35] Erich Fromm and Michael Maccoby mention some of the games included here with respect to female weakness and male strength. See Fromm and Maccoby, *Social Character in a Mexican Village* (Englewood Cliffs, New Jersey, 1970), 146–147.

[36] Collected from María Pilar Gómez, 22, Guanajuato, Gto., México, who learned it from playmates when a child. See also Mendoza, 95.

"*La monjita*," or The Little Nun, is a popular *rondo* in Mexico that originated in Spain.[37] In its longer versions it is a *romance*, or ballad. This game speaks of the arbitrary way families, particularly in the past, determined whom a young girl married: the father chose the husband for the girl. The practice still occurs in Mexico but less frequently. If the girl had the courage to refuse to marry the man chosen for her by her family or, even worse, dared to pick a man of her own liking, woe be unto her! She might be severely harassed, threatened, or even beaten into submission. One form of punishment in the past if all else failed, particularly in Spain and Portugal, was to lock up the recalcitrant girl in a convent. "*La monjita*" sadly and poignantly expresses just such a situation.

The girls form a circle with one girl, *la monjita*, in the center. They clap softly while they sing, and the little nun pantomimes the actions of the song.

La monjita

Yo me quería casar
con un mocito barbero
y mis padres me querían
monjita del monasterio.

Una tarde de verano
me sacaron de paseo
y al revolver una esquina
estaba el convento abierto.

Salieron todas las monjas
todas vestidas de negro,
me agarraron de la mano
y me metieron adentro.

Me empezaron a quitar
los adornos de mi cuerpo:
pulseritas de mis manos,
anillitos de mis dedos,
pendientes de mis orejas,

. . . .

Lo que más sentía yo
era mi mata de pelo[38]

. . . .

[I wanted to marry a young barber, and my family wanted me to be a nun in a monastery. One afternoon in springtime, they took me for a walk and on turning a corner, there was an open convent. All the nuns came out, all dressed in black. They took me

---

[37] *Romances populares y vulgares*, Biblioteca de escritores de Chile, vol. 7 (Barcelona, 1912), 175–176.

[38] This version is taken from Mendoza's *Lírica infantil*, 126. He calls it "*Yo me quería casar*" ("I Wanted To Marry"). I collected a shorter version from Paula Rángel Márques, 40, Guanajuato, Gto., México, who learned it from her mother. See also *Canciones de España y América* (Madrid, 1965), 20.

by the hand and pulled me inside. They began to remove the adornments from my body; bracelets from my arms, rings from my fingers, earrings from my ears. . . . But what made me most sad; they cut off my hair. . . .]

If a woman's individuality is suppressed, if her right to dignity and freedom is taken from her, if her life is made a punishment, she is going to be a destructive creature, for she will seek ways of getting back, directly and indirectly, consciously or unconsciously, at those who harm her. She has done this throughout the centuries, and the Mexican woman is no different in this respect from her sisters throughout the world who are not allowed to live their lives in dignity. Women in such cultures become most destructive, in my opinion, when they are old. For example, when a son marries, sometimes the mother in the Mexican folk culture will behave divisively, trying to cause conflict between the new bride and the son.[39] Furthermore, she is often harsh with the new daughter-in-law, demanding that she perform heavy and unnecessary household duties. Here is a game Mexican girls play that blatantly, humorously, and realistically tells about this situation. Notice at the end how the mother turns to the son with divisive tactics and notice his exasperated response. Notice also the daughter-in-law's cheekiness; one wonders whether many young women are so daring in this culture. As the game is sung it is enacted like a little play. It is called *"La suegra y la nuera"* ("The Mother-in-law and The Daughter-in-law"). Mendoza states that this game appears to have evolved in Mexico.[40]

La suegra y la nuera

Suegra: M'hijo se casó, ya tiene mujer.
          Mañana veremos lo que sabe hacer.
          Levántate, mi alma, como es de costumbre,
          Lavar tu brasero y poner la lumbre.

Nuera: Yo no me casé para trabajar,
          Si en mi casa tengo criados que mandar.

Suegra: ¡Demonio de nuera! ¿pues qué sabe hacer?
          Coja usted la escoba, póngase a barrer.

Nuera: ¡Demonio de vieja! ¿por qué me regaña?
          El diablo se pare en sus sucias marañas.

Suegra: ¡Demonio de nuera! ¿pues qué sabe hacer?
          Coja usted la aguja, póngase a coser.

Nuera: ¡Demonio de vieja! ¿por qué me maldice?
          El diablo se pare en sus sucias narices.

Suegra: Yo quise a mi nuera, la quise y la adoro,
          por verla sentada en las llaves de un toro.

Nuera: Yo quise a mi suegra, la quise y la quiero,
          por verla sentada en un hormiguero.

[39] Kiev, 110–111.
[40] Mendoza, 17.

Suegra: Ay, ay, ay, ay, ay, que me haces llorar,
          con los malos ratos que me haces pasar.

Nuera: Ay, ay, ay, ay, ay, que me hacen llorar
          las ingratitudes que me hacen pasar.

Suegra: ¡Ay, hijo de mi alma, mira a tu mujer!
          Llévala al infierno, no la puedo ver.

Hijo: ¡Ay, madre del alma, cállese por Dios!
          Que yo ya me canso de oír a las dos.[41]

[*Suegra*: My son has married, now he has a wife. Tomorrow we will see what she knows how to do. Get up, my soul, it is customary for you to wash the hearth and light the fire. *Nuera*: I didn't get married to work; in my house I have servants to order around. *Suegra*: Devil daughter-in-law! Well, what does she know how to do? Get the broom and sweep. *Nuera*: Devil old woman! Why do you quarrel with me? May the devil stop in your dirty tangled hair. *Suegra*: Devil daughter-in-law! Well, what do you know how to do? Get the needle and sew. *Nuera*: Devil mother-in-law! Why do you curse me? May the devil stop on your dirty nose. *Suegra*: I love my daughter-in-law. I love her and adore her, to see her seated on the horns of a bull. *Nuera*: I love my mother-in-law. I love her and adore her, to see her seated on an ant hill. *Suegra*: Ay, ay, ay, ay, ay! You make me cry. You give me such a bad time. *Nuera*: Ay, ay, ay, ay, ay! The ingratitudes I receive make me cry. *Suegra*: Ay, son of my soul. Look at your wife. Take her to hell. I can't stand her! *Hijo*: Ay, mother of my soul. In God's name be quiet! I am tired of the two of you.]

Finally, I found two games in Mexico in which girls play at being dead. The one that follows is a *rondo*, another singing game. Very slowly the girls circle holding hands. One girl, representing death, is in the center. She chooses another to take her place as they sing out the sad tale. It is called "*La Muerte*" ("Death").

La Muerte

Naranja dulce, limón celeste,
dile a María que no se acueste.

María, María, ya se acostó,
vino la Muerte y se la llevó.

Naranja dulce, limón silvestre,
dile a mi amada que me conteste.

María, María, no contestó,
vino la Muerte y se la llevó.[42]

[Sweet orange, celestial lemon. Tell María not to go to bed. María, María, has already gone to bed; Death came and took her away. Sweet orange, unripe lemon. Tell my beloved to answer me. María, María, does not reply; Death came and took her away.]

---

[41] Ibid., 126–128.

[42] Collected from María Pilar Gómez, 22, Guanajuato, Gto., México, who learned it from playmates when a child. See also Mendoza, 95.

It is significant that a man is ordering the woman to come to him and that her refusal to come takes the form of death. Perhaps this is the only way a woman can refuse to obey a man in such a culture—by dying. The melody of this little *rondo* is very pretty, despite the somber meaning, but I don't think children are very often found playing games of death.

None of the women who gave me these games was aware of the symbolic meaning inherent in them until it was pointed out. The women generally stated that they remembered the games because of their pretty melodies and because singing and playing them brought joy to their lives. This appreciation of their charm is important. Games, like other expressive folk forms, persist because they reflect and give expression to values, beliefs, and attitudes of a culture but also because they fulfill other needs which are just as important; these games Mexican girls play are vitally alive today and have persisted not only because they may give expression to feelings of frustration, hostility, and fear, but also because they are artistic expressions that are aesthetically satisfying.

Only a few games are presented here, although others exist which reflect the situation I have described.[43] Mexican women share most of these games with their Spanish and Portuguese sisters, for the majority of the games originated in centuries past in the Iberian Peninsula and reflect a common restrictive and paternalistic attitude toward women that has persisted for centuries in all Spanish and Portuguese cultures.[44]

If games children play can sometimes be regarded as rehearsal for adult life, then these games played by Mexican girls, along with their Spanish and Portuguese sisters, predict a very dreary adulthood indeed.

APPENDIX

Musical Examples

Maria Blanca

---

[43] For example, *La viudita* and *Hilitos de oro*.

[44] Countless *romances* may be found which speak to this situation. See Ramón Menéndez Pidal, *Los romances de América* (Madrid, 1958); Almeida Garrett, *Romanceiro*, 3 vols. (Lisboa, 1963); *Revista Lusitania* (Lisboa, 1895), vol. 3; *Romancero General*, 2 vols. (Madrid, 1947); Carolina Michaelis de Vasconcellos, *Romances velhos em Portugal* (Coimbra, 1934); Rossini Tavares de Lima, *Romanceiro folclorico do Brasil* (São Paulo, 1971); and *Romances populares y vulgares*, vol. 7.

Naranja dulce

La monjita

La suegra y la nuera

La Muerte

"A Helpmate for Man Indeed"

The Image of the Frontier Woman

BEVERLY J. STOELTJE

THE VERY NATURE OF THE "FRONTIER," in any geographical setting, implies a process of adaptation in the settlement of that frontier, an interaction of the settling people with the physical environment. New settlements also involve, however, the interaction of the settlers with each other in the new environment, through which interaction a new or modified society is established. In this social adaptation process, behavior forms are drawn from cultural images already in the possession of the individuals who are adapting. These images are then modified or new ones created which will conform to the demands of the environment or situation. Because the process is an interaction of images, behavior, and environment, the resulting forms may have numerous variations, may exist for an unpredictable period of time, and will exhibit *degrees* of success and failure along a continuum, the extreme poles of which are defined by survival or extinction.

This article approaches the American frontier as an adaptive process and examines specifically the roles of women during the settlement period of the frontier. The American "frontier" refers here to the occupation and settlement by Euro-Americans of territories in the United States that were previously unoccupied by such groups. The nineteenth century, particularly the latter half, is the time focus, and the Southwest and Midwest are the particular geographical areas given the most consideration. The aim is not to establish an objective, "real" description of everyday life on the frontier, but to formulate and test a hypothesis regarding symbolic frontier woman. The basic questions regarding frontier women are: What were the images of women possessed by the settlers when they arrived on the frontier? How were these adapted to the frontier? What is the symbolic representation of frontier women?

The major components of the social adaptation process are images (the symbolic representations), behavior, and environment. The environmental influences are perhaps the easiest to identify: climate, resources, distance from settlements, and other physical characteristics. Behavior and images are much more difficult to distinguish. Images influence behavior, behavior will ultimately influence images, and environment will influence both at the same time. In addition, written descriptions or artistic-literary expressions of experience, authored both by participants and by observers, contemporary or historical, will be influenced by the images they possess. There are, then, a symbolic environment—the possessed images—and a physical environment which influence the behavior. The result of the interaction between the two is the adaptation process. However, though these interactions move toward adaptation, they may move also in a maladaptive direction due to a disjunction of the symbolic and physical environments or of several symbolic environments. Because human experience constitutes the data the adaptation process must utilize, the maladaptive influences will be related to those experiences for which there is no mechanism that can transform them into cultural positives. It is through the encounters of experience, possessed images, and evolving images that the universe is restructured by members of the culture. However, restructuring does not equate with removal, because symbols and images that have been transformed into negative value forms may be maintained, though maladaptive, as part of the mechanism for organizing the culture until cultureogenesis has been accomplished. Once restructuring has been accomplished and evidence of culture change is apparent, the conflict between symbols and value systems does not necessarily cease, but the dominant position is assumed by new symbols and images. The continued existence of opposing sets of symbols and values lies at the source of much of the expressive behavior of a culture, such as we find in comedy and tragedy.

The data considered here illustrate the symbolic process in transformation. Images of women are brought by the settling people to a new environment, the frontier, where adaptation must occur. The images must undergo transformation, each acquiring new qualities of autonomy and value within the new environment; then a new set of relations between them develops, and a symbolic representation of frontier women can be identified. It is hoped that this article will reveal something about the cultural position of women in frontier society by means of an inventory of cultural images. The inventory does not claim to be exhaustive but rather is an outline of images within which variations can occur and from which some conclusions can be drawn about the symbol "frontier woman."

Because the frontier was first settled by men it is possible to note the changes brought about by the introduction of women. Women brought institutionalized "civilization" to the "wilderness." Though the forms of institutionalization were skeletal—social occasions, funerals, religious instruction, and the like—many participants and observers recognized that women assumed responsibility for them. Their roles became established within the new environment, and values and emotions were expected to conform to these roles. In this process of interaction between the demanding physical environment and the social environment, a transformation was effected through which a modified image of women emerged.

The following hypotheses are set out to suggest how the frontier experience affected the image of women's cultural role in America: (1) due to the environmental demands of the frontier, women's roles were changed on the behavioral level from those roles practiced in "civilization"; (2) cultural *images* and *symbols* had to be transformed and adapted, and the division of labor redefined; and (3) therefore, the opportunities for change in women's roles available on the frontier were limited to a great extent so that the symbol system would not disturb the general order. However, the symbolic frontier woman is not a clear case of change or no-change; the implications of the frontier experience for her are two-directional. The demands made on frontier women presented new situations and thus opportunity for new means of expression because society's structures were not so rigid as those in areas already settled.

Three types of frontier female images and three types of frontier male images emerge as dominant: (1) the refined lady, (2) the helpmate, and (3) the bad woman; and (1) the cowboy, (2) the settler, and (3) the bad man. It is necessary to consider the male roles as well as the female roles, for the male-female association determines a great part of either role within the society. These roles will be discussed in terms of a distance-sexuality element that defines the relationship between the male and female roles. In the first "set" of roles—the cowboy and the refined lady—distance between the male and female is great, and little if any sexuality is expressed in the relationship. The settler and the helpmate occupy the same household, but sexuality is given narrow recognition in the roles, which focus primarily on reproduction with emphasis on division of labor. The bad woman and the bad man association recognizes sexuality as the primary basis for the relationship. However, they occupy the same space for brief periods of time only. Each of these roles occupies a position in the inventory of images ranging from an idealized vision of chaste woman based on great distance to a "sinful" but exciting image based on close but temporary contact, the midpoint of the inventory being characterized by close contact with nonrecognition of sexuality. This inventory constitutes the primary images available to women on the frontier, though variations were possible.

The first symbolic male type is the cowboy. He is of particular importance if we accept Boatright's view that the cowboy symbolizes man's conquest of nature and the last frontiersman.[1] The cowboy is characterized by his horse, membership in an all-male group, alcohol (whiskey), loneliness, contact with the raw elements and animals, mobility, honor, sometimes a pistol, sometimes a fiddle. The cowboy possessed an idealized image of women, though he was more likely to spend time with prostitutes than with his "ideal." His contact with women frequently came in the "city" at the end of the trail drive or, as the frontier became more settled and more women arrived, at ranches where dances were held. These contacts were generally brief and infrequent. The cowboy's ideal woman was a chaste, beautiful, princesslike, fragile creature, set apart from the real world upon a pedestal where he could worship her from afar. The cowboys were frequently labeled "the boys." This labeling implies that they have not assumed the responsibilities of "men" by settling down with their own ranch and a woman; when they did settle down, they became "cattlemen." As

[1] "The American Rodeo," *The American Quarterly*, 16 (1964), 202.

"boys" they had not reached maturity in civilization terms and, therefore, maintained a boylike relationship to women—worship from afar of an unattainable princess.

One cowboy who rode the cattle trails in Texas and Oklahoma in the 1880's, J. W. Kennedy, wrote the following verses in his journal:

> You are an angel and a blessing, O darling how I love you.
> Unto you I give my whole possessions, Rewarding you for
>   proving true.
> Can you so hard and cruel be Unto the passions of my heart
> Not to permit me at your feet to kneel.
>
> In after years
> When this you see,
> I wonder what your name will be.   (Jan. 11, 1889)
>
> When I am in some far and distant land, and other friends
>   around you stand,
> Let not my absence brake the tie that binds the hearts of you
>   and I.
>
> Dear old girl
> How I love you
> No laddie knows.
>
> Love is sweet, but o how bitter to love a girl and then can't
>   get her.
>
> Let all your care be cast a way like dew
> Before the sun and when you have nothing else to do
> Just think of me for fun.

This view of women certainly was not unique to the cowboy; in fact, it illustrates how much the cowboy used the literary stereotype of the time.

Cowboys were often described as shy around women, and some were known to have a complete aversion to women. In a historical account of the settlement of Northwest Texas, Josie Baird says, "Although the boys appreciated and respected the women of the area, they were often very shy around them. Charley Binnion, the roper without peer, would not speak to a woman if he could prevent it, and Doc Shultz was an avowed woman hater. These two were courteous, however, when they could not avoid women."[2]

An anecdote that appeared in a collection of cowboy lore illustrates a common attitude toward male-female relationships. In the story, entitled "Bud's Letter," a group of cowboys in 1883 had left the Grayson County Ranch, and Bud Wallace was the only boy in the outfit to leave a girl behind. The rest of the boys were not so fortunate or unfortunate as to have girls. Bud and his girl agreed to write to each other, and he received letters at each post office. When he wrote to the girl about having to drive through Indian Territory, he received a letter

2 Josie Baird, "Ranching on the Two Circles Bar," *Panhandle Plains Historical Review*, vol. 18 (Canyon, Texas, 1944), 56.

from her, which he did not share with the group as was the custom; however, the cook read the letter and had a big laugh. The other "boys" then managed to read it as follows:

"Now dear Bud, in your letter you spoke of going among those horrid old Indians. Now dear Bud, don't let those Indians kill you for you know if should they I would die for dear Bud, you know that you are the pork and beans of my soul and the roasting ears of my heart."

Two days later if we wanted peace in camp it was best not to mention pork and beans or roasting ears.[3]

The intensity of the reaction to the letter and the fact that the incident entered into oral tradition and then into print provide an indication of the unusual nature of this event. Were such letters the routine for cowboys, it is unlikely that the letter would have received such attention, which suggests that direct communication between the sexes of a romantic nature (whatever the specifics of the metaphor) was not the norm.

In discussing the frontier hero, not just the cowboy, John G. Cawelti tells us:

Reluctance with words often matches the hero's reluctance toward women. . . . At other periods, writers have tried to make a romantic hero out of the cowboy, as in Wister's *The Virginian* and the many novels of Zane Grey. However, even when the hero does get the girl, the clash between the hero's adherence to the "code of the West" and the heroine's commitment to domesticity, social success, or other genteel values usually plays a role in the story. Heroes such as the Lone Ranger tend to avoid romance altogether. They are occasionally pursued by women, but generally manage to evade their clutches.[4]

Thus the symbolic cowboy who appears in early documents, movies, songs, and novels did not have a female counterpart in reality, generally. Some cowboys possessed an image of an idealized, genteel woman, and others avoided the idea of women completely, or claimed to. Though the cowboys visited the houses of prostitution, in that context they were temporarily transformed into the role of "bad man." There are then two cowboys: the romantic but shy cowboy and the disaffected cowboy.

The first type of female under consideration here is the "refined lady" of a sensitive, emotional nature. The genteel woman who appeared in some cowboys' verses and song did occasionally appear on the frontier but seldom adjusted to the frontier unless she altered her refined ways to some extent. Descriptions of these genteel ladies appear in regional histories and novels. If they refused to adapt their refined ways to the environment, they suffered unhappiness or extinction. "Mrs. Tom Adair who came from Atlanta, Georgia, as a bride, could not become adjusted to dugout life. The men on the ranch teased Tom by telling him that he would have to blindfold his wife and back her into a dugout in order to get her to live in one. Mrs. Adair admits that she never enjoyed living in a dugout, because she was never able to keep anything clean."[5] Another

---

[3] *Spur Jingles and Saddle Songs, Rhymes and Miscellany of the Cow Camp and Cattle Trails in the Early 80's* (Amarillo, Texas, 1935), 26.

[4] *The Six-Gun Mystique* (Bowling Green, Ohio, 1971), 27.

[5] Baird, 47.

woman from the Deep South married a man also from the South who moved to West Texas.

To him, so far removed from his proper surroundings, she became more than a mere wife; she was the symbol, as well, of everything he held dear in the life he had left behind; a combination of those virtues from which springs all that is good and beautiful, and of those social graces, which according to his aristocratic standard, were the outward expression of inward perfection. Therefore, unlike most husbands, he had no desire to mold her to suit either his needs or the ways of the country to which he had brought her.[6]

However, her brother-in-law had another view of the situation: "only an extravagant woman from the improvident South would make *dogies* of three poor calves just because she wanted cream and cake with her afternoon tea."[7] (Apparently three range cows were kept to supply milk for the lady's tea, their calves becoming motherless at her expense.) This same woman, because of her husband's "thoughtfulness" in permitting her to go unmolded to the environment, never adjusted to frontier life. Lewis comments, "The years before her widowhood were too filled with happiness for her to contemplate seriously on the outcome to one of her kind of a life in the West. By the time the realization came it was too late . . . she was an old woman, alone in the land of which she had so steadfastly refused to become a part."[8] Describing the wife of Charles Goodnight, the same author (a woman) states, "To one and all she stood for everything that is admirable in womanhood, this gentle 'lady' from Tennessee. Set by circumstances amid surroundings too uncongenial to her highstrung, sensitive temperament, she was dashed and buffeted by the winds of western life till her frail body broke."[9] Another refined lady who came to the Texas Panhandle in frontier days was the wife of a doctor. Dr. Stocking was at first reluctant to migrate because of his worry that his wife would not be accorded the treatment to which she was accustomed. The doctor was persuaded to come, but his wife died within a year following the move.[10]

In Lewis' opinion the frontier had an inviting as well as an austere side, and the hardships were encountered with more ease than the "spiritual confusion of today." This was especially true for women, she feels, "except in rare cases where their natures were such that fear and loneliness had disastrous effects on their emotional balance."[11] The environment was one which placed hardships on women, and some women, especially the gentle lady types, were not able to adapt to these conditions. Barbara Welter has explored the image of this gentle lady type as it appeared in women's popular literature between 1820–1860. She defines the four cardinal virtues of "true womanhood" as piety, purity, submissiveness, and domesticity. "Put them all together and they spelled mother, daughter, sister, wife—woman. Without them, no matter whether there was fame, achievement or wealth, all was ashes. With them she was promised

[6] Willie Newbury Lewis, *Between Sun and Sod* (Clarendon, Texas, 1938), 195.
[7] Ibid.
[8] Ibid., 194.
[9] Ibid., 57.
[10] Ibid., 176–177.
[11] Ibid., 141.

happiness and power."[12] This was the image of woman many settlers brought to the frontier, both male and female. Although some elements of this image proved useful in the new environment, more strength and initiative were required—thus those who could not adapt "broke," either physically or emotionally, from the strain.

This leads to consideration of the second type of male—the settler, the man who brought the refined lady to the frontier. ("Settler" is used to refer to both cattlemen and farmers who had families and owned land—those who established permanency in a region and usually started families.) Charles Goodnight, the giant of the Plains, exemplifies the cattleman of this type. He is described by Lewis as

abounding in vitality, intelligent, a keen observer of every manifestation of Nature and a gifted judge of men and cattle. His outstanding characteristics were physical endurance, an aptitude for work, self-confidence, and determination. . . . He was the essence of rugged individualism, the type of pioneer most admired by the American masses. . . . He and his kind laid the foundation for an empire, it is true, but without conscious effort, while engrossed upon their own selfish concerns. . . . Therefore, in view of this and also the confusion of many contradictory opinions, it is difficult to know whether Goodnight was "a bighearted diamond in the rough whose uncouth exterior gave little evidence of the keen intelligence and sterling character underneath" or "an overbearing master, unpopular with the cowboys, who was the finest fellow in the world as long as one did exactly as he desired; whose one ambition was to rule the Plains country, and who, at one time, came near doing it" or, as his chief champion described him, "a great man with a simple nature and the frontier's foremost stockman."[13]

This aggressive, ambitious, self-confident man who tackles the frontier and succeeds in every effort but has a delicate, sensitive wife who does not adapt to the frontier is reminiscent of *Giants in the Earth*, the novel of Norwegian immigrants who settled in Dakota Territory. Per Hansa, the frontier hero of the novel, tackles the frontier with success in every venture. He is described as having "that indomitable, conquering mood which seemed to give him the right of way wherever he went, whatever he did."[14] His neighbors are amazed at his energy and achievements in building the first house, breaking the most land, having successful crops, and generally overcoming obstacles and creating abundance in spite of difficulties. His wife, Beret, however, draws increasingly into a world of darkness, unable to relate to Per Hansa, the neighbors, or the children. She comes to believe that "this desolation out here called forth all that was evil in human nature," and that their coming had been a mistake. Her own feelings were of fear: "She was only afraid—afraid . . . a timid child in a dark room."[15] Though Per Hansa adores his wife and brings her wonderful gifts from the wilderness he conquered, she finds no solace in her position upon a pedestal and gradually withdraws into her own private world. At first she had been fascinated with her role. Memories from her courtship were expressed by her as, "All was nothing as compared with this great certainty. . . . Ah, no—

[12] Welter, "The Cult of True Womanhood: 1820–1860," *American Quarterly*, 18 (1966), 152.
[13] Lewis, 56–57.
[14] O. E. Rolvaag, *Giants in the Earth* (New York, 1955), 41.
[15] Ibid., 279.

she knew it well enough: for him she was the only princess!"[16] Per Hansa, however, does not share his ideas with her but rather fulfills them and presents them to her completed. Because of her fear she makes no attempt to participate in the environment, and the two draw apart—she into her fear and loneliness and he into the environment.

As the above example illustrates, it is possible to find elaboration of the details of the refined lady's experience in literary expression of the frontier experience. Although *Giants in the Earth* is also an account of an immigrant experience, it is most especially an encounter of settling people with the environment. Per Hansa thrives on his encounters with Nature while Beret withdraws from life in the absence of civilization and institutions. In her inability to transform her images, she fails to adapt.

The second type of woman under consideration, the helpmate, is the woman who successfully adapted to the frontier conditions. The primary distinction between this woman and the refined lady is in the strength and initiative exhibited in coping with the hardships and the demands of the life they led. Her strength was physical and emotional. She was able to carry out routine, everyday chores of milking, cooking, sewing, gardening, caring for chickens, childbearing and childrearing, caring for the sick, and generally acting as partner with her husband. Such women were equally adept at handling emergency situations—Indian attacks, droughts, death. Individual women made specialized contributions such as reading Bible stories or holding "open house" for the young people to see their pretty "things," but the primary defining feature of this group of women was their ability to fulfill their duties which enabled their men to succeed, and to handle crises with competence and without complaint. The image of the woman who fulfilled this role has roots in the "backwoods belle" of the Old Southwest. Boatright describes this image as it appeared in the Davy Crockett almanacs, which we may consider as part of mass art, as follows:

The backwoodsman never made womanhood a cult, and while he was just as quick to fight as any man if he felt that the honor of an individual woman was involved, he made no grandiose defense of womanhood as such. . . . By a process of inversion in which he was adept, ugliness, uncouthness, and "unladylike" strength and demeanor were so exaggerated that they could not be taken seriously. Thus he created a laugh and showed his contempt for leisure-class standards of femininity. . . . The result was a considerable body of traditional lore, preserved by oral transmission and by early newspapers, but chiefly by a series of David Crockett almanacs published from 1835 to 1856.[17]

Though the backwoods belle was hefty, grotesque, and mean with a pistol, she was not without a tender side. She was fond of pets and went to hear the circuit rider when he came and made him welcome.[18] "She was known all the way from the Allegheny to the Rocky Mountains. She was always on hand 'with heart, arms, and pockets open.' She wore out 'seven of her nine constitutions and used up four consumptions and seven fever agues in saving travellers from

---

[16] Ibid., 217.
[17] Mody Boatright, *Folk Laughter on the American Frontier* (New York, 1961), 44.
[18] Ibid., 52.

freezin', famine, wolves and vultures.' " This backwoods belle was a "worthy helpmate to her husband."[19] Crockett's wife did many chores to help him, including turning the grindstone for him when he wanted to sharpen his thumbnail and providing eggnog on Easter, even if it involved trouble for herself.[20] This image of a superwoman who is extremely capable but expects so little for herself is best described in the almanac as follows:

The greatest example of wifely devotion of all was Katy Whippoween. She brought up a "smart chance of children" with no expense to their father except for their education. . . . thar war a lady what took a young bear to bring up and to be treated as one of the family, and Katy offered to taik it to nuss till it got big enuff to feed. In this way she arned enuff to keep her husband in whiskey. . . . But she got nothing for her panes, for all her children turned out bad. One of im is a minister.[21]

Even though these sketches in the almanacs are meant to be humorous, several traits of the early symbolic frontier woman emerge as characteristic. She
  (1.) was strong and tough;
  (2.) took responsibility for the welfare of others;
  (3.) had a variety of skills which she used often;
  (4.) provided for husband's and children's needs;
  (5.) expected no help or reciprocation;
  (6.) was a helpmate to her husband;
  (7.) was highly valued by men for the above qualities, for they did not value the leisure class standards of femininity.

In other sources women display strength, but, as the frontier moves further west and further into the nineteenth century, it requires of women not only brute physical strength but the ability to bear up under difficulties as well. One such woman who displayed this strength and the ability to cope was Sarah Hornsby of Texas. She appears in a legend recorded by J. Frank Dobie. Though a refined lady, to judge from her background, she was not afraid of the frontier and exhibited the bravery and initiative so admired on the frontier. Thus she illustrates the transformation process: she combines elements of the images of the refined lady and of the backwoods belle in order to meet the demands of the environment. Dobie entitles the legend "The Dream That Saved Wilbarger." In the legend Sarah Hornsby has a dream that Josiah Wilbarger, a neighbor, did not die when scalped by the Indians, as witnesses believed. She insists that the witnesses and her husband return to the site and bring Wilbarger to safety. Though two men who witnessed the scalping assure her that Wilbarger is dead, she convinces her husband that her dream is true. She and the children will be in danger when the men leave, but she says, "Never mind me, I and my children can take to the dogwood thicket and lie hid. Go, I tell you, to poor Wilbarger."[22] Dobie describes this determined woman as "a little, black-haired, black-eyed woman of pure Scotch blood off a plantation of traditional refinement in Mississippi. She sang Highland ballads, read the Bible to her children, and taught

---

[19] Ibid., 53.
[20] Ibid.
[21] Ibid., 54.
[22] Dobie, *Tales of Old-Time Texas* (Boston, 1955), 38.

them to read the box of books she had hauled in an ox wagon all the way to Texas."[23] Yet her delicacy does not inhibit her bravery. In her husband's absence she frightens away Indians by dressing in men's clothing and appearing with a rifle; she and her young sons later bury young men she witnessed being killed by Indians, and she herself buries one of her own sons killed by Indians.[24]

In his memoirs John Holland Jenkins describes frontier women in Central Texas of the mid-nineteenth century as follows:

the girls were so strong and fine and healthy-looking and they seemed so wide-awake and earnest. Their waists were not so waspish nor their bustles so large as they are today. . . . They were raised on bear and buffalo meat and venison and wild honey with plenty of good pure fresh air and work to do. . . . And our girls knew how to weave and spin and churn and do anything that came along there. . . . Fashion meant common sense and economy and comfort. . . . I believe the women here now are as pretty and fair as can be found, but they do not look so healthy and comfortable and happy, and I do not see many who look like they could pass through what Mary Jane and others of our veteran ladies of Bastrop County have endured.[25]

James Wilson Nichols, 1820–1887, describes the bravery of several women of Central Texas, near Fredericksburg, in his journal. One story involves the Henry M. Day family. Mrs. Day leaped from the wagon with one child in her arms when the Indians attacked. Though she was wounded, she risked her life further and returned to the wagon, just as it was being driven away by the Indians, to snatch her other child, "and made good her retreat back to her tree and other child amid loud yells and a shower of arrows and bullets . . . the woman hesitated not a moment to imperil her own life for that of her child."[26]

In another instance, Mrs. Friend was both scalped and wounded in the thigh but crawled a mile and a half in the snow and north wind to reach her home because she was "very ankcious to know the fate of her little ones at home."[27] (Her husband found her unconscious at the gate upon his return home at midnight.) Nichols states, "Now me thinks the heroism, bravery and deturmination of these three women has never been surpased in anciant or modern history or the bravery and deturmination and example set fourth by these females ever been equeled in this age of the world."[28]

In Parker County, near Weatherford, Texas, in the latter half of the nineteenth century there was great concern in the rural churches over the woman's position in the church. One member maintained that women should not take part in church business, since they did not possess a soul. One "free-thinker," however, "dared to advance the theory that if a man had a soul, it was reason-

[23] Ibid.

[24] Ibid.

[25] John Holmes Jenkins, III, ed., *Recollections of Early Texas: The Memoirs of John Holland Jenkins* (Austin, 1958), 210–211.

[26] Catherine W. McDowell, ed., *Now You Hear My Horn: The Journal of James Wilson Nichols, 1820–1887* (Austin, 1967), 163.

[27] Ibid., 165.

[28] Ibid., 166.

able to presume that a woman had one too."[29] At any rate, in the town of Weatherford the question of a woman's soul did not prevent the churches from "letting the women help pay for their new brick or frame buildings." The county historian, H. Smythe, wrote: "For nearly ten years an effort has been made to rear a house of worship for the Christian denomination. Attempts by man signally failed; the women magnificently accomplished their purpose." They accomplished this through needle work and knitting appliances and two public festival entertainments.[30]

We learn from this author also that a woman's role was specifically defined, both by the women as well as the men. And in this role, she was held responsible for her marriage and was expected to do an excellent job of her chores.

Gossip, of course, was one of the chief pasttimes. Women sometimes stepped off the straight and narrow path, and wise heads nodded thereafter. If a woman separated from her husband, she usually was blamed for the marital failure, but if she were any part a lady, she would not further disgrace herself by getting a divorce. A more grievous plight than ever was for a woman to fail to get married before she was twenty-five. No one in his senses would marry an old maid of twenty-five or past. Women liked to talk about the slovens in their neighborhood—triflin', they called them. Why, they made butter with cow tracks in it, it was so vile smelling. They couldn't make an apple pie bed. They stitched their selvage seams together instead of whipping them. Their spinning rolls were bull tails, bulky and not suitable for the making of good thread. They were the kind of people who had no turkey-red embroidery on white pillowshams, who let the fire go out, who had to borrow soft soap, who didn't keep the weevils out of their seed peas, who let their gourds get soggy.[31]

Life further west in Fisher, Scurry, Kent, and Stonewall counties, Texas, is described by Josie Baird. She says of the pioneer women,

These pioneer women were as strong as their husbands in their desire to make new homes in the isolated section. For the most part they bore the hardships without complaint but they did dislike the sandstorms, dugouts, and the lack of water. . . . Despite the hardships most women who came to the ranch stayed and made the best of the situation. . . . They brought about significant changes in the lives of the cowboys. Though the cowboy made jokes concerning the settlers, they enjoyed their changed social existence. Women were added to annual ranch barbecues where platforms were built for dancing, and everyone ate and danced and drank most of the day and night.[32]

Though never stated clearly, it was only the men who drank, and whiskey was their drink.

Besides creating a social life where none existed before, women brought about other changes in frontier life.

Mrs. Greenwood tried to bring some of the culture of her earlier home into the lives of the cowboys. While she was living on the ranch, a bronc fell with Lee Shultz and killed him. Mrs. Greenwood held a funeral service for him. The boys remembered that service, for religious services of any kind were very unusual. Even though most of the boys admitted

[29] Afton Wynn, "Pioneer Folk Ways," in *Straight Texas*, ed. J. F. Dobie (Hatboro, Pennsylvania, 1966), 197.
[30] Ibid.
[31] Ibid., 233.
[32] Baird, 56–57.

that the ranch was no place for women, they were happy that some women were willing to make their homes on the ranches.[33]

A most interesting example is provided by Mary Taylor Bunton in her story *A Bride on the Old Chisholm Trail in 1886.* Originally from Austin, this young woman, who had a formal education and had traveled widely, exemplified the role of refined lady. She then married a rancher from Nolan County (West Texas). She eagerly moved to the frontier and, as her decision to accompany her husband on a trail drive up the Chisholm Trail shows, adopted traits of the backwoods belle. Though it was required that women make difficult trips across rough country when moving to the frontier, it was unheard of for a woman to go on a trail drive. This was a male domain and not a family venture; women were not permitted under any circumstances. After word was out that Mary was indeed going on the drive, relatives and friends came to Mr. Bunton and said,

Look here, young man, we have come out here to give you a talk straight from the shoulder, and we are not going to mince words with you either. To tell you the truth, the whole truth, and nothing but the truth, all of us think you have lost your mind. It's the craziest idea we ever hear of—your promising to take Mrs. Bunton with you on this trip up the trail. You ought to realize that she is too young, too inexperienced, and too unaccustomed to hardships of any kind to make such a trip, and she is a bride, besides. Why, man, even to let her start the trip with you will likely end in tragedy. Think it over, and you had better heed our warning.[34]

Then they appealed to Mary herself, saying that they were surprised that she would want to "add the care" of herself to her husband's responsibilities.

Mary insisted on going on the trip, however, and rode all the way to Coolidge, Kansas. She established herself after killing a rattlesnake and cutting off the rattles. She was then considered a "seasoned veteran" rather than a "tenderfoot."[35] This example, though not typical of most women, exhibits most obviously the transformation from refined lady to helpmate.

Most important, therefore, is Mrs. Bunton's conclusion to her story, in which she does not emphasize herself and her independence but rather her role as her husband's helpmate: "Howell Bunton was proud of the record his young wife had made and as long as he lived he paid highest tribute to her courage and wifely devotion—truly a helpmate for man indeed."[36] This helpmate concept also appears in other sources. Willie Newbury Lewis, a female writer, describes the wife of one of Goodnight's neighbors, Thomas Sherman Bugbee (no name is given for the wife): "His wife was only a blue-eyed, quick-tempered, laughing girl, so small she could stand under her husband's outstretched arm, but she made a perfect complement to the big, steady, taciturn pioneer, and it was the two together who brought to success the Quarter Circle T."[37]

The ability to endure pain and hardship was valued whether they were per-

---

[33] Ibid., 56.
[34] *A Bride on the Old Chisholm Trail* (San Antonio, 1939), 29.
[35] Ibid., 41.
[36] Ibid., 71.
[37] Lewis, 61.

sonal or environmental. A young woman in the Clarendon community fainted and fell into an open fire during an epileptic attack. Though the burns were fatal, "During her last agonies, she spoke only once, then to apologize for the screams which she, in her pain, had been unable to suppress."[38]

In the same community an economical and literal woman went to visit the doctor to have a tooth extracted. He, being unskilled as a dentist, jokingly commented, "If it does *not* hurt, *I'll* not *charge* you a cent." She sat in the chair "without movement or change of expression until he had finished, . . . arose, straightened her clothes, thanked him and walked out. The matter of a fee was never mentioned by either."[39]

Bravery and endurance in women were highly valued on the frontier. Emotional expression between the sexes or in any form, however, seems rare and was valued only when successfully repressed. Larry McMurtry states in "Eros in Archer County" that we have little in the way of recorded conversations or other data to tell us about communication between the sexes.[40] The data suggest that expressions of affection and love were restricted to the romantic cowboy mentioned earlier. Actual relationships between the sexes are described more as partnerships than as romances. The following anecdote is provided as an example. "There were amusing incidents, sometimes even in the presence of death, as when the old Dutchman looked into the face of his deceased wife and said, 'Doc, I believe it would have been easier for me to give up my best span of mules than that old woman.' "[41] Though this statement is made in humor, it also tells us that the closest the speaker can come to expressing love for his deceased wife is to compare her to his best mules.

Some further indication of communication between the sexes can be obtained from Edward Baxter Featherston's report of his courtship with his wife. Featherston was a pioneer in West Texas in the late nineteenth century. A friend suggested to him that Bettie Moxley might marry him if he approached her and acted "sensible." He "went to courting" Bettie, and they wrote letters every two weeks. In one letter he proposes marriage as follows: "If you are willing to marry me when I come home this fall, show this letter to your father." He continues, "In due time the answer came back, 'Pa has seen your letter.' We were married at her father's house November 27, 1874."[42]

Featherston's wife complained at times, according to his report, that her husband did not court her enough, but when he would offer, she would say, "I don't want any of your foolishness now."[43] Though he states that he feels "courting" a woman is very important, his evidence indicates that only a minimum of "courting" ever occurred. He gives his evaluation of his wife as follows: "Her economy and industry enabled me to make an honest living and raise our family. When I consider the quality of our offsprings I am abundantly sat-

---

[38] Ibid., 178.
[39] Ibid.
[40] *In a Narrow Grave* (Austin, 1968), 19.
[41] Lewis, 179.
[42] Featherston, *A Pioneer Speaks*, ed. Vera Featherston (Dallas, 1940), 58.
[43] Ibid.

isfied."[44] Though the author may have had other feelings about his wife as well as these, if we consider his report a "transcript" of the culture, a term used by Kenneth Boulding to describe a communication which is in some sense independent of the communicator but which conforms to tradition in its selection of messages, we can consider economy and industry that help the husband, plus producing "quality" offspring, the valued traits of the frontier woman.[45] His comments on their communication further illustrate that communication was minimal on the subject of romance and courtship.

Relationships of males with females and communication between the two are described in the going-to-bed rituals of a pioneer family in Parker County.

Going to bed was a delicately handled ceremony in the large families. The children washed their feet in the summer time, and were properly dressed in their night garments and tucked away in the trundles. When it came time for the grown-ups to retire, the men all went outside to give a last look to the stock while the women undressed. The men returned to find the women all in bed. Candles were then extinguished and the men undressed in the dark. The coals were banked in ashes for the night, and on cold mornings the head of the household arose, slipped on his jeans and built the fire. Usually the men arose first and went to see about the stock while the women dressed.[46]

Distance, then, was imposed between the sexes in frontier families even in close living quarters, even in winter.

In the first category of frontier males, then, is the cowboy—the alienated, disaffected cowboy who is an avowed hater of women or the romantic cowboy who dreams of princesses and love but has little or no contact with such women. In these cases the male either remains a member of his male group, the "boys," never taking a wife, or perhaps he marries late in life to a woman whom he places upon a pedestal. In the second male category is the landowner who marries and settles permanently in the area, giving up the mobility of the cowboy. He is frequently a cattleman, though in some regions of the frontier he is a landowning farmer. If he marries the first type of woman under consideration, he is marrying the cowboy's dream, the "refined lady," the epitome of "true womanhood." This female is too sensitive and emotional to weather the hardships of the frontier and either dies or becomes emotionally imbalanced. The male is successful in his role as a frontiersman; the female is a failure as a frontier woman because she cannot adapt to the frontier, by becoming a helpmate. If the male marries the second type of woman, the helpmate, they will be "successful," for she will adapt to the role of a strong, enduring, nonsexual helper for the cattleman-settler.

A third image on the frontier was the "bad woman." She appears in a variety of forms, generally associated with sex and raw Nature. The role of bad woman was certainly not created on the frontier, but in adapting to the conditions of the frontier it assumed a prominent and special position there. In frontier areas where there were trading relations with Indians it was not unusual for white males to avail themselves of the Indian "squaws" during trading periods, as

44 Ibid., 59.
45 *The Image* (Ann Arbor, 1964), 54.
46 Wynn, 205.

contrasted to the Indian princess who had to be won and married. *The Big Sky*[47] has both these roles clearly defined, and, as with the refined woman above, the marriage of the hero with the Indian princess ends in disaster. In the Anglo setting bad women were especially associated with saloons, dance halls, alcohol, and rowdy living. Some frontier towns were largely built around this culture. One such town on the Texas plains was Tascosa,

a typical boom town characterized by "bad men, prostitutes, revolver shots and whiskey," in perfect accord with the "relentless hardness" of the surrounding region and the unstable quality of the ephemeral era which produced it. Its population was a colorful aggregation of humanity, cowboys with six-shooters, senoritas in lace mantillas, priests in robe and cross, university graduates, gamblers and desperadoes, whose chief place of amusement went under the fitting but offensive name of "Hogtown" and was marked by a sign which read "no shooting beyond this line."[48]

A customer could enter the large adobe building that housed this area through the business quarters, that is, "the door of respectability," and then proceed to the bar and the dance hall. "The queen of the district was 'Rowdy Kate' and her accomplices went by such descriptive titles as Rag-Time Annie, Drowsy Dollie, Crippled Callie, Box-Car Jane, Panhandle Nan, Fickle Flossie, Old Ella and Midnight Rose."[49] In addition to these women there was Mrs. Betty Trube, who ran the "eating house." She was as strong as a man and wore a six-shooter, which she did not hesitate to brandish if anyone threatened the peace in her establishment. Creole Mary, also known as Frenchy, was the partner of the best-known gambler, a jovial Irishman from Dodge City. The legend goes that she "was the shrewdest monte-dealer in the West," and "night after night she sat among the other sports dressed in her red shoes, spangled blouse and patchwork skirt, with rarely a word except to her 'talking canary.' "

In his novel *Leaving Cheyenne* McMurtry offers a description of a bad woman.[50] Though Molly is not a prostitute, she is not a part of acceptable society. She is wife to her husband, an oil field worker, and lover to a cowboy and also to a cattleman. The cowboy has no wife, the cattleman has a wife, but both express their love and passion with Molly, emotions that should have been kept hidden, if not completely repressed. Certainly Molly would qualify as a frontier woman in her ability to endure hardship. However, the more acceptable frontier woman must be a helpmate to a husband and must be devoid of passion. Molly qualifies on neither score. As a product of a literary work representative of the internal literature of the region Molly is more complex than some of the images provided by the earlier "transcripts," but she is nevertheless defined as the embodiment of sexuality and thus resides beyond acceptable society.

The "bad man" constitutes the third type of male. Since he has already been much discussed as a social bandit, a Robin Hood, and a hero in many instances, there is no need to discuss the type in detail. Billy the Kid and Jesse James represent typical bad men or outlaws, though it must be remembered that many

---

[47] A. B. Guthrie, *The Big Sky* (Boston, 1947).
[48] Lewis, 59.
[49] Ibid.
[50] New York, 1963.

cowboys and respectable men could be bad men when they chose to visit the saloons and bad women, their respectable roles being reassumed upon return to the ranch or home. The bad men also lived outside the margins of society and did not conform to the code of "civilization" or participate in the institutional life of society—thus they were the natural partners of the bad women. Their endeavors did not require that the female partner be a helpmate, and a working partner, but that the female be available for temporary periods of time when the male's activity brought him into her presence. The bad woman, then, was also subject to the male role for a definition of the female image.

Given the demands of the environment, the refined lady image in its pure form could not survive. A transformation from female to nonsexual comrade was necessary. Perhaps the only woman who survived as a female was the bad woman. The bad woman and the bad man, however, lived beyond the margins of society, as so aptly implied in the name of the district "Hogtown" of Tascosa, an animal town, not for civilized people. Fiedler, Cawelti, and McMurtry have emphasized the all-male society of the code of the West. As McMurtry states, this is not a suggestion of repressed homosexuality but rather an indication of repressed heterosexuality.[51] There is no place for expression of passion or affection between the sexes within the society. Relations between sexes *within* society were based on a nineteenth-century idealization of woman, who was to be treated with "honor" and politeness but without emotion by the cowboy or as a comrade who is a nonsexual partner by the settler type. For passionate, heterosexual relations on the frontier, one must look beyond institutionalized society to the wilderness, inhabited by animals and bad women and bad men. Even here, however, it is the male who has choices and determines the nature of the relationship in terms of time and distance.

The symbolic transformation of images of women that took place on the frontier involved the following initial images: (1) the refined lady symbolizing "true womanhood," defined by Eastern, literary civilization and bringing with her the elements of formal institutionalization—education, religion, "high culture"; (2) the "backwoods belle" (the opposite of the delicate, refined lady), who could accomplish fantastic deeds involving strength and capability and had the ability to establish informal elements of institutionalization, in particular the family; and (3) the bad woman, found outside the boundaries of society and in association with sex and sin. These images of women were related to the following male images: (1) the cowboy, mobile, unsettled, and idealistic about women or alienated from them; (2) the cattleman-settler, the aggressive domineering man who conquered the frontier or the wilderness with great success; and (3) the bad man, the outlaw, who operated beyond respectable society.

In the adaptation to the frontier environment, physical and social, these female images were modified or underscored. The refined lady could survive only if she assumed some of the strength of the backwoods belle. The bad woman was easily accessible in many frontier towns, and the association of gambling, alcohol, and general rowdiness further emphasized the "bad" in the bad woman.

[51] *In a Narrow Grave*, 72.

The helpmate, who drew from the backwoods belle image yet combined elements from the refined lady in some cases, successfully responded to the demands of frontier living, which required that she possess bravery, strength, and initiative as well as the ability to establish and nurture institutions. In this interaction of images and environment, the environment forced the refined lady image into a maladaptive position in the paradigm. In the adaptive position certain opportunities were made available to women, as exhibited by Mary Bunton. However, the biological role of women and the cultural division of labor curtailed these opportunities. More important, however, the symbol of woman that evolved as the successful frontier woman contained its own limitations. The more capable the woman, the more successful in adapting she was, the more the woman assumed the comrade position. The comrade was nonsexual and found identity by association with the cattleman-settler. As Mary Bunton stated it, she was "truly a helpmate for man indeed." The expression of emotion and passion was delegated to the bad woman, whose identity was not tied to an association with a respectable man (at least not recognizably) and who was generally single and lived in the margins somewhere between animals and people. Her image, however, was also primarily defined by the male counterpart.

Thus through the symbolic transformation process evolved a symbolic frontier woman who was above all capable of managing basic institutions, of bringing civilization to the frontier. She had economy and industry, which enabled her man to be a success. Because the refined lady and bad woman images led to failure or exclusion from society, they could not be considered successful in attaining the goal of survival within the new society. The strong, capable, institutional, comrade woman then became established as the symbolic frontier woman, for this image had the capacity to survive within frontier society. However, since maladaptive symbols may remain within a symbol system, the refined lady and the bad woman images also persisted.

If America does indeed identify itself with the frontier experience, if some regions still practice "symbolic frontiersmanship," as several scholars have suggested, then a study of contemporary American images available to women might well begin with an examination of the symbolic frontier woman and the process by which this image became established as an institution in itself.

Things Walt Disney Never Told Us*

KAY STONE

THE FOLLOWING ITEM appeared recently in a Winnipeg newspaper:

In Pittsburgh, Pennsylvania, a burglar lost his shoe as he fled from the home of Mrs. M., age 43. Patrolmen arrested R. T., age 20, who was sitting shoeless in a nearby bar. Authorities said a shoe matching the one found in the M. home was discovered behind the bar.[1]

The headline read, "Police Use Cinderella Approach." This brief example is only one of many that illustrate the popularity of fairy-tale heroines in North America. That they are household words as well as "household tales" is attributable to the unintentional efforts of the Grimms and the very intentional efforts of Walt Disney.

Despite the wide appeal of such heroines, they have received little scholarly discussion. Stith Thompson's definition of the term *Märchen* begins by stating that the genre is characterized by "such tales as 'Cinderella,' 'Snow White,' or 'Hansel and Gretel,' "[2] but he then goes on to consider only the exploits of *Märchen* heroes. Lord Raglan does not include a single heroine in his international survey of twenty-one heroic characters.[3] Linda Dégh explains that she has excluded most heroines from *Folktales of Hungary* because they are much the same throughout Europe; it is only the heroes who take on national coloring.[4] In North America, where oral forms of the *Märchen* are not abundant and where the Grimm tales are read mainly by or to children, heroines have been virtually ignored except by a handful of writers interested in children's literature.[5]

---

* I thank all those who have offered suggestions on this article, especially Claire Farrer and Linda Dégh.

[1] *Winnipeg Free Press*, April 14, 1972.

[2] *The Folktale* (New York, 1946), 8.

[3] *The Hero* (New York, 1956), chap. 16.

[4] Chicago, 1965, xxx.

[5] See, for example, Marcia Lieberman, "Some Day My Prince Will Come," *College English* (December, 1972), 383–395; Alison Lurie, "Fairy Tale Liberation," *The New York Review of Books* (December 17, 1970), 42–44; and "Witches and Fairies: Fitzgerald to Updike," *The New York Review of Books* (December 2, 1971), 6–8. Sporadic references to fairy-tale heroines are found in Simone de Beauvoir, *The Second Sex* (New York, 1953), and Betty Friedan, *The Feminine Mystique* (New York, 1963).

In attempting to correct this imbalance in attention I have surveyed both popular and scholarly collections in English and have asked dozens of women to recall their childhood memories. Almost all of those interviewed were completely unfamiliar with Anglo-American heroines, most of whom appear in scholarly collections not often found in children's sections of libraries. All, however, could easily recall tales popularized through the numerous Grimm translations and the Disney films.[6] These tales are so thoroughly accepted that one woman even referred to the Grimm stories as "English fairy tales," because her German-born mother told her "real" (German) tales.[7]

What have the Grimm translations offered to North American children? Of the total of 210 stories in the complete edition, there are 40 heroines, not all of them passive and pretty. Very few translations offer more than twenty-five tales, and thus only a handful of heroines is usually included. Most of them run the gamut from mildly abused to severely persecuted. In fact, a dozen docile heroines are the overwhelming favorites, reappearing in book after book from the mid-nineteenth century to the present.[8] Cinderella (AT 510A) and Frau Holle (AT 480) succeed because of their excessive kindness and patience; Sleeping Beauty (AT 410) and Snow White (AT 709) are so passive that they have to be reawakened to life by a man; and the innocent heroines of "The Little Goose Girl" (AT 533) and "The Six Swans" (AT 451) are the victims of scheming and ambitious women.

The villains are not always women, however. A girl is forced by her father to accept a grotesque suitor in "The Frog Prince" (AT 440), and another is married off to a greedy king by her father in "Rumpelstiltskin" (AT 500). Still another father is encouraged by his daughter to mutilate her in order to save himself in "The Girl Without Hands" (AT 706). Though this tale is not quite as popular as the others, it is sufficiently well known to have inspired author Joyce Carol Oates's newest novel.[9]

Some Grimm heroines do show a bit of spirit, but they are not usually rewarded for it. In "The Clever Peasant Lass" (AT 875) the girl is threatened with abandonment by her boorish husband, and the proud daughter in "King Thrushbeard" (AT 900) is humbled by both her father and her unwanted husband. Only Gretel ("Hansel and Gretel," AT 327) is allowed a brief moment of violence in order to save herself and her brother. No other popular Grimm heroines destroy the villain.

The passivity of these heroines is magnified by the fact that their stories jump

[6] The impact of the Grimms in England and North America is detailed in Katharine Briggs, "The Influence of the Brothers Grimm in England," and Wayland Hand, "Die Märchen der Brüder Grimms in den Vereinigten Staaten," *Hessische Blätter für Volkskunde*, 54 (1963), 511–524 and 525–544.

[7] R. R., interviewed in Winnipeg, January 3, 1973.

[8] These are, in order of their popularity: "Sleeping Beauty," "Snow White," "Cinderella," "Rapunzel," "The Frog Prince," "Hansel and Gretel," "Rumpelstiltskin," "King Thrushbeard," "The Little Goose Girl," "Red Riding Hood," "Frau Holle," and "The Six Swans." AT numbers in this article refer to type numbers from Antti Aarne and Stith Thompson, *The Types of the Folktale*, Folklore Fellows Communications No. 74 (Helsinki, 1928).

[9] *Do With Me What You Will* (New York, 1973). The title is taken from the girl's words to her father.

from twenty percent in the original Grimm collection to as much as seventy-five percent in many children's books. In this sense the fairy tale, a male-oriented genre in Europe (both by tale and by teller), becomes a female-oriented genre in North American children's literature.

But if the Grimm heroines are, for the most part, uninspiring, those of Walt Disney seem barely alive. In fact, two of them hardly manage to stay awake. Disney produced three films based on *Märchen* ("Sleeping Beauty" and "Snow White" from the Grimms and "Cinderella" from Perrault). All three had passive, pretty heroines, and all three had female villains, thus strongly reinforcing the already popular stereotype of the innocent beauty victimized by the wicked villainess. In fact, only half of the Grimm heroine tales have female villains, and among the Anglo-American tales, only one-third. Yet even Stith Thompson believes otherwise; he states that "for some reason, to the composer of folktales, it is the woman of the family who is nearly always chosen for the part of the villain."[10]

But Walt Disney is responsible not only for amplifying the stereotype of good versus bad women suggested by the children's books based on the Grimms, he must also be criticized for his portrayal of a cloying fantasy world filled with cute little beings existing among pretty flowers and singing animals. Though a recent magazine article calls him a "Master of Fantasy," in fact Disney has removed most of the powerful fantasy of the *Märchen* and replaced it with false magic.[11]

In brief, the popularized heroines of the Grimms and Disney are not only passive and pretty, but also unusually patient, obedient, industrious, and quiet. A woman who failed to be any of these could not become a heroine. Even Cinderella has to do no more than put on dirty rags to conceal herself completely. She is a heroine only when properly cleaned and dressed.

In contrast, *Märchen* heroes can be slovenly, unattractive, and lazy, and their success will not be affected. The Grimms' "Hans-my-Hedgehog" (AT 441) has a hero who actively exploits his grotesque shape in order to gain power, wealth, and—of course—a beautiful wife. The hero of "The Little Red Ox" (AT 511A), unlike his passive sister in "One-Eye, Two-Eyes, Three-Eyes" (AT 511), does not docilely accept his fate: he kills his stepmother instead of the helpful ox and rides boldly away. The many youngest-son tales known as "male Cinderellas" almost always have heroes who, unlike the female Cinderella, do not seem to be the least bothered by their unfavored position. One of these, in the Grimms' "The Youth Who Wanted to Learn What Fear Is" (AT 326), is clearly described as dull and stupid, in contrast to his clever and industrious brother. He is seen as a burden to the family because he does everything wrong. Not exactly the typical Cinderella. The only resemblance between this hero and Cinderella is that he wins in the end because he proves to be more courageous than his brother, not because he sits home awaiting the arrival of a princess.

---

[10] Thompson, 113.
[11] "The World That Disney Built," *Newsweek* (October 15, 1973), 101–102.

Heroes succeed because they act, not because they are. They are judged not by their appearance or inherent sweet nature but by their ability to overcome obstacles, even if these obstacles are defects in their own characters. Heroines are not allowed any defects, nor are they required to develop, since they are already perfect. The only tests of most heroines require nothing beyond what they are born with: a beautiful face, tiny feet, or a pleasing temperament. At least that is what we learn from the translations of the Grimm tales, and especially from Walt Disney.

To judge from the 186 heroines found in five major Anglo-American folktale collections, oral narrators do not confine themselves to passive princesses.[12] There are even women who express a national coloring apparently lacking in European heroines. England has a female version of "Jack and the Beanstalk," for example, and the United States has several heroines well suited to a tough pioneering life. They do not always rely on sympathetic fairy godmothers or overprotective dwarfs, nor do they always await the last-minute arrival of the hero. And, as already mentioned, they are more often aggravated by male villains than by the familiar wicked stepmother.[13]

Among the Ozark tales collected by Vance Randolph, we find women who destroy the threatening male villains and also a girl who does not need her father to convince her that frogs make interesting bedfellows.[14] Leonard Roberts introduces a number of Kentucky heroines who do not fit European stereotypes. The heroine of his version of "Cupid and Psyche" (AT 425A) marries a prizefighter instead of a more obvious beast and is not intimidated by his brutal treatment.[15] In "The Little Girl and the Giant" (AT 327) a mother and daughter cooperate in escaping from a giant and destroying him.[16] The Randolph and Roberts collections, and others also, offer a number of versions of "Cinderella" (both AT 510A and 510B) that would have made Disney's hair curl.

Four British heroines are outstanding. One ("Kate Crackernuts," AT 306 and 711), in an unusual version of "The Twelve Dancing Princesses," not only rescues a prince from nocturnal fairies but also cures the beautiful stepsister deformed by the heroine's own jealous mother.[17] Another, in "Mossycoat" (AT 510B), leaves home voluntarily—with the encouragement of a loving mother, not because of the threats of an incestuous father.[18] Unlike many of her counter-

---

[12] Katharine Briggs, *A Dictionary of British Folktales*, vol. 1 (London, 1970); Marie Campbell, *Tales from the Cloud Walking Country* (Bloomington, Indiana, 1958); Emelyn Gardner, *Folklore from the Scholarie Hills, New York* (Ann Arbor, Michigan, 1937); Vance Randolph, *The Devil's Pretty Daughter* (New York, 1955), *Sticks in the Knapsack* (New York, 1958), *The Talking Turtle* (New York, 1957), and *Who Blowed Up the Church House?* (New York, 1952); and Leonard Roberts, *Old Greasybeard* (Detroit, 1959), *South from Hell-fer-Sartin* (Lexington, Kentucky, 1955), and *Up Cutshin and Down Greasy* (Lexington, Kentucky, 1959).

[13] Of the 186 heroine tales, only 62—exactly one-third—had exclusively female villains. Of the male villains, many were angry fathers, murderous lovers, and jealous husbands.

[14] Vengeful heroines are found in abundance in *The Devil's Pretty Daughter*: "What Candy Ashcraft Done," 6; "How Toodie Fixed Old Grunt," 63; and "The Girl and the Road Agent," 139. In the same volume is "The Toad-frog," 91.

[15] "Bully Bornes," *South from Hell-fer-Sartin*, 60–63.

[16] Ibid., 45–46.

[17] Briggs, *A Dictionary*, 344.

[18] Ibid., 416.

parts, she is not only unintimidated by her jealous fellow-workers, but actually bewitches them into silence.

Still another heroine (in "Tib and the Old Witch," AT 328) leaves home in protest over her father's rejection of her lover.[19] She is not locked in a tower as in the Grimms' "Lady Madelaine" (AT 510A), nor is she forced to choose against her will as in "King Thrushbeard." Neither does she return home after her adventures to live happily ever after.

Even more aggressive is the heroine of "Mally Whuppee" (AT 328).[20] She also leaves home, but with two sisters whom she protects from a giant and for whom she wins husbands before she wins one for herself. She earns them by answering a king's challenge to return and steal the giant's treasures. Unlike Jack ("The Boy Steals the Giant's Treasures," AT 328), she succeeds in doing so without killing the giant. She even prevents him from unknowingly destroying his own wife. A more violent American version of the same tale has the heroine in competition with her sisters, who want to kill her, and more violent toward the giant; she does not destroy him but does drown his wife.[21]

In none of these tales do we find the stereotyped conflict between the passive, beautiful woman and the aggressive, ugly one. Most of the active heroines are not even described in terms of their natural attributes—and Mally Whuppee is presented as less attractive than her stepsister. Like heroes, they are judged by their actions. Though most do marry, their weddings are no more central to the tale than is the concluding marriage of most heroes. Some husbands are even won as passive prizes, in the same way that princesses are won by heroes in many tales. Most important, active heroines are not victims of hostile forces beyond their control but are, instead, challengers who confront the world rather than waiting for success to fall at their pretty feet. Unfortunately, heroines of this sort are not numerous in oral tales and do not exist at all in any of the Grimm tales or the Disney films.

Female aggressiveness is not the only aspect of heroine tales that is unfamiliar to most of us. Sexuality in fairy tales seems to be limited to Jack's beanstalk.[22] Overt sexual references, if they even find their way into original collections, rarely appear in children's books. Translations of the Grimms, for example, usually omit the fact that Rapunzel's initial encounter with the prince resulted in twins. The Grimms' "other" Cinderella, "All-Kinds-of-Fur" (AT 510B), is usually left out altogether, since the heroine is forced to leave home to avoid her father's threats of an incestuous marriage. A "Disney version" of this tale is difficult to imagine, for Disney found even the more passive Grimm version of Cinderella (AT 510A) unsuitable for children and used the more innocuous Perrault version instead.

Other sexual references are more subtle. We must look closely to discover that it is at puberty that Rapunzel is locked in a tower, Snow White is sent out to

19 Ibid., 522.
20 Ibid., 400.
21 "Polly, Nancy, and Muncimeg," in Roberts, *Up Cutshin and Down Greasy*, 119–123.
22 See Alan Dundes, *The Study of Folklore* (Englewood Cliffs, New Jersey, 1969), 107–113, for two examples of phallic interpretation of "Jack and the Beanstalk."

be murdered, and Sleeping Beauty put to sleep. Such heroines have their freedom severely restricted at a time in life when heroes are discovering full independence and increased power. Restrictions on girls at puberty, in contrast to the increased freedom their brothers enjoy, possibly explain the intensely sympathetic reaction many women have to such passive heroines in fairy tales.[23] In the specific tales mentioned, this restriction reflects anxiety about competition with other women that increased sexuality offers. It might also be seen as a protection for the heroine herself, who must remain pure for the one man who will eventually claim her. The restriction of women at puberty can also be interpreted as a reaction of men to the threat of female sexuality.[24]

Though female symbols in general have certainly been considered by Freud, Jung, and a handful of other scholars, they still lack a familiar name, and, compared with phallic symbols, have received practically no attention from folktale scholars.[25]

As Freud notes, female symbols are those that suggest the possibility of either entry or entrapment. These would include rooms and houses, ovens, jugs and bowls, shoes, and forests and flowers. Such symbols do not appear randomly or without meaning. They take their significance from the context in which they are used; thus it is not necessary to interpret every house, for example, as a female symbol. Occasionally the symbolism is obvious, such as the hero's plucking of the enchanted flower in AT 407, "The Girl as Flower." Other references are more obscure—the fitting of Cinderella's slipper in AT 510A or her ring in AT 510B.[26]

Both male and female symbols can be portrayed positively or negatively, reflecting either desire or anxiety. In this sense Jack's powerful beanstalk leading to a treasure contrasts sharply with the imposing tower in "Rapunzel" or with the dagger used to murder Bluebeard's wives in some versions of AT 312. Similarly, the lovely enchanted flower presents quite a different image than does the threatening witch's hut or the magic forest, both of which trap unwary male travelers.[27] It is Hansel, one remembers, who is trapped first in the witch's hut and then in her cage.

Sexuality is also portrayed as harmful to the heroine herself. There are many symbolic hints that women should not become too familiar with their own bodies. Bluebeard's wives are murdered for looking into forbidden rooms, and Sleeping Beauty is punished with near death from a sharp object for doing so. Other heroines are threatened with death for breaking a tabu against looking into a fireplace in versions of AT 480 ("The Kind and the Unkind Girls"), and little

---

[23] V. S., interviewed in Winnipeg, May 3, 1973.

[24] See, for example, H. R. Hays, *The Dangerous Sex* (Richmond Hills, Ontario, 1964), especially chap. 4.

[25] See, for example: Sigmund Freud, *A General Introduction To Psychoanalysis* (New York, 1969), 156–177; Carl Jung, *The Collected Works of C. G. Jung*, vol. 9, part I (Princeton, New Jersey, 1968); and Lewis Mumford, *The City in History* (Harmondsworth, Middlesex, England, 1961), 15–17.

[26] For a provocative interpretation of Cinderella and female sexuality, see Lea Kavablum, *Cinderella: Radical Feminist, Alchemist* (Guttenberg, New Jersey: privately printed, 1973).

[27] See, for example, Hays, 148.

girls are murdered by their stepmothers for breaking jugs in several versions of AT 720 ("The Juniper Tree").

Sexual imagery of this sort would not be obvious to most children (or to most adults), but some writers feel that fairy tales do satisfy a more general psychological need, at least for North American children. They suggest that children might view themselves as the helpless underdogs who eventually triumph over the powerful witches and ogres representing their parents.[28] Michael Hornyansky emphasizes that North American children are still avid readers of fairy tales, possibly because of such identification: "The stories they want to hear last thing at night . . . are 'Sleeping Beauty,' 'Red Riding Hood,' 'Cinderella,' 'Snow White,' 'Jack and the Beanstalk,' and that crowd: stories full of princes, princesses, giants, wicked witches, wolves, dwarfs, and other persons not normally encountered."[29]

Hornyansky mentions only one hero tale, thus underlining the observation made earlier in this paper that the large number of heroine tales in fairy-tale books indicates that these are meant for girls. It does not seem an exaggeration to say, as one feminist writer does, that fairy tales may serve as "training manuals" in passive behavior, and that "Millions of women must surely have formed their ideas of what they could or could not accomplish, what sort of behavior would be rewarded, and of the nature of reward itself, in part from their favorite fairy stories. These stories have been made the repositories of the dreams, hopes, and fantasies of generations of girls."[30] A popular psychiatrist, the late Eric Berne, felt that fairy tales offer not only dreams and hopes but actual programs for behavior. Your favorite fairy tale may parallel and inform your attitudes and acts.[31]

Rather than accept these views uncritically, I interviewed forty women of varying ages and backgrounds.[32] All had read fairy tales, almost all could name several favorite heroines but rarely any heroes, and most of these tales were from Disney or the Grimms. Many admitted that they were certainly influenced by their reading of fairy tales. Some had openly admired the lovely princesses and hoped to imitate them—especially their ability to obtain a man and a suburban castle without much effort. An eleven-year-old told me, "I thought I'd just sit around and get all this money. I used to think 'Cinderella' should be *my* story."[33] Another admirer of Cinderella, a nine-year-old, said, "Well, I wouldn't really want to marry a prince like she did—just somebody *like* a prince."[34]

Others reluctantly admired the passive princess because there were few alter-

---

[28] See, for example, Eric Berne, *What Do You Say After You Say Hello?* (New York, 1973), especially chap. 3; Bruno Bettelheim, "Bringing Up Children" (monthly column), *Ladies' Home Journal* (October and November, 1973); Michael Hornyansky, "The Truth of Fables," *Only Connect*, ed. Sheila Egoff and others (Toronto, 1969), 121–132.

[29] Hornyansky, 121.

[30] Lieberman, 385.

[31] Berne, chaps. 3, 12, and 13.

[32] Interviews were conducted in Miami, Minneapolis, and Winnipeg, from December, 1972, to August, 1973. The ages of the women ranged from seven to sixty-one.

[33] R. S., Winnipeg, June 13, 1973.

[34] C. C., Miami, December 25, 1972.

native images, but they did not expect to imitate either her attributes or her material successes. Said a twenty-nine-year-old:

I remember the feeling of being left out in fairy stories. Whatever the story was about, it wasn't about *me*. But this feeling didn't make me not interested in them—I knew there was something I was supposed to do to fit in but I didn't. So I thought there was something wrong with *me*, not with the fairy stories.[35]

A twenty-four-year-old told me that she had really expected to bloom one day as Cinderella had done, but she was still waiting.[36]

Many of those who admired the passive princess, either openly or reluctantly, recognized her image in various forms of popular entertainment, notably in romantic tales on television and in comic books, magazines, and novels read almost exclusively by women. Even women who had shaken the persistent princess in their daily lives returned to her in fantasy through such popular materials. The woman who mentioned feeling left out in fairy stories said she had to force herself to stop buying romantic magazines: "They depressed me and made me feel confused. There was something about them—something like the victimized fairy-tale women—that I didn't want to see in myself."[37]

Many informants under the age of fifteen (the post-Disney generation) were not so impressed with the passive heroines of Disney and the Grimms. Some found them boring and stopped reading fairy tales altogether, such as the young woman who said, "That poor princess, so beautiful and helpless. She sure will have a long wait for that prince to show up!"[38] Others who liked the fantasy world of the *Märchen* claimed they compensated for the lack of interesting heroines by reading about heroes, but they could rarely name even one.

Still others performed a fascinating feat of selective memory by transforming relatively passive heroines into active ones. Several were mentioned (including the persecuted sister of AT 451, "The Maiden Who Seeks Her Brothers"), but the best remembered was Gretel, who pushes the witch into the oven. In fact, this is her only aggressive act, and it seems almost accidental in comparison with those of the ever-confident Hansel. He does not even lose hope when he is caged but devises the fake finger to fool the witch into delaying his death. Yet not surprisingly it is the tearful Gretel who is remembered by girls in search of active heroines, for Gretel is indeed aggressive when compared with most of the Grimm heroines and *all* of the Disney heroines. However, when contrasted with the Anglo-American heroines mentioned earlier, she seems far less heroic. We see through her what we have lost by taking our heroines from Grimm and Disney, rather than from the tales of our own heritage.

Among the informants, whether they admired Cinderella or found her boring, whether they felt heroines like Gretel were active or were not, there was general agreement that considerably more diversity would have been welcome. Many reacted favorably to a rewritten version of AT 300 ("The Dragon-Slayer"), in

[35] L. J., Winnipeg, January 6, 1973.
[36] S. L., Winnipeg, January 26, 1973.
[37] L. J., of n. 35.
[38] L. M., Miami, December 22, 1972.

which an unintimidated princess destroys her own dragon and leaves the men to clean up the remains.[39] All were interested to hear that there were even traditional heroines—and Anglo-American ones at that—who were equally impressive. Walt Disney neglected to tell us that Cinderella's freedom does not always end at midnight.

[39] Jay Williams, "The Practical Princess," *Ms.* (August, 1972), 61–64. Another "liberated" tale by the same author is "Petronella," *McCall's* (January, 1973), 74–110.

The Native Costumes of the Oberwallis

Tourist Gimmick or Tradition?

AGNES FREUDENBERG HOSTETTLER

HIGH ABOVE THE RHONE VALLEY, surrounded by snow-covered mountains and glaciers, lies the village of Saas-Fee. Five hundred seventy adults over twenty-one years old, half of them women, live here. Sports of the area—winter and summer snow-skiing, skating, sleigh riding, swimming, and mountain climbing—were enjoyed by over seven thousand tourists last year. Yet only twenty-two years ago no road led to the village, only two paths, one for mules and one for people. Tourists came only during the very short summer season of six weeks in July and August. Rugged mountain farming, raising sheep, goats, a few cows, some barley and rye provided most of the daily needs of the people. The women helped shear the sheep, and they spun and wove the wool for their families' clothes, knitted socks and stockings, and rented the spare room to tourists in the summer. It was a hard life because all labor was manual. For instance, they had to cut the hay with scythes and sickles along the steep mountain sides and carry it down on their backs. Because most men were guides in the summer, the women did this work, as well as milking the cows and goats.

Women wore plain, long, black skirts and jackets, dark aprons, and yellow or black head scarves. For Sundays and holidays, they had the brighter colored aprons and shawls around their shoulders. The most original item of their native costume, the *Kreshuet*, a small straw hat with a *Krause* or *Kres* (a black silk ribbon pleated into hundreds of tiny folds around the rim and a wide beautifully embroidered black or white silk or velvet ribbon pinned to the top), had all but disappeared. Julie Heierli writes in her book *Die Volkstrachten von Bern, Freiburg und Wallis* that during the inauguration of a new priest in Almagell (near Saas-Fee) in 1925, not a single woman wore a hat; all wore scarves. In the same year, at the Ascension Day celebration in Saas-Fee, only twelve of more than a hundred women had on hats, all of which were old, some from the 1860's.[1] In contrast, in 1973, for the Corpus Christi procession

---

[1] *Die Volkstrachten von Bern, Freiburg und Wallis*, vol. 2 (Zürich: Eugen Rentsch Verlag A.G., 1927), 160. Permission to reprint the photographs in Plates 1–5 and 7 is gratefully acknowledged.

in Saas-Grund, all but a handful of several hundred native women wore their white- or black-ribboned hats with the traditional costumes. The question arises: Why did the wearing of the native costumes and in particular the *Kreshuet* make such a spectacular comeback? Did tourism have anything to do with it? If so, was it a negative or positive influence?

I found the reason for the decline in the wearing of native costume in Julie Heierli's book. In Goms, a village at the end of the Rhone valley, the hat disappeared after the building of a railroad which brought tourists up to the mountain valley.[2] The tourists paid so much attention to the women's hats that these self-conscious ladies felt embarrassed and left them in their closets. The same happened in other villages of the Oberwallis: the women were reluctant to conform to their native traditions in the face of staring outsiders.

The turning point of regaining their pride as Swiss women came in the thirties when Hitler took power in Germany and Mussolini in Italy. Located between the Nazis and the Fascists, the Swiss became more and more aware of their own national heritage. When the Swiss National Fair, the *Landesausstellung*, opened in Zürich in 1939, there were beautiful exhibits of folk art, folk crafts, and costumes. The Second World War, in which Switzerland was almost completely cut off by the Nazis and Fascists, helped create a deeper sense of patriotism—a returning to the almost four-hundred-year-old roots of the democracy, to its folkways and traditions, which included the women's native costumes.

In the case of Saas-Fee, a further development that provided impetus was the building of the road, which brought tourists and money to the village. Now the women could afford to have new costumes and hats made. They were proud to be different, and they wore their native costumes with the hats for all holidays and many Sundays.

Wanting to find out the women's responses to a revival of tradition, I posed the following questions in January, 1973, to eighteen women between twenty and seventy years of age: Do you own a native costume? Do you still wear it and why? Do you belong to the *Trachtenverein* (a local group of women owning native costumes)? To the first question, all but one answered "yes." The exception was a local woman born in Basel who felt that because she was not born in the Wallis she should not wear its costume. Of the seventeen who owned a native dress and hat, all but two wore them regularly. Of those two, one said it made her look older than her twenty-five years, the other thought she was too fat for it. When asked why they wore these costumes, the women said that they found them pretty or beautiful, that they enjoyed wearing them and did not mind the money spent for them.

The fifteen women wore their costumes on all those Sundays designated as *Trachtensonntage* by the *Trachtenverein* and for holidays, processions, baptism, communion, the *Sängerfest* (song festival), and other folk festivals to which they were invited as a group, accompanied by the village band. All fifteen women belonged to the *Trachtenverein*; the one in Saas-Fee was formed in the

[2] Ibid., 160.

1950's, the Saas-Grund group only four years ago. The *Trachtenverein* is a purely social group, which meets once a month. One of its goals is to keep alive the costume tradition and to pass it on to the young girls. The dresses, aprons, and jackets are all made by one seamstress in Saas-Grund. The black shawls are imported from the Bretagne, where they also are part of the native costumes. But the crucial item is the *Kreshuet*, which is the most original part of the complete outfit.

Until about five years ago, nobody in Saas-Fee or Saas-Grund remembered how to make the *Kreshuet*. Each hat still worn was old, at least the straw part of it, which had been hand pleated from local straw and sewn together to form a plain, flat, little hat with a small rim. Only one woman, in her sixties, remembered how to pleat the straw bands. She began making the hats, and her daughter, Antonia, decided to teach herself to make the *Kres*, the black silk ribbon that has to be folded in hundreds of tiny pleats to fit around the rim of the hat. Antonia has lived all her thirty-five years in Saas-Grund. She is also one of four women who still own and use their weaving looms. During the quiet months of October and November she does a great deal of weaving. Ten years ago, she said, there were still forty women weaving in Saas-Grund, but today, with tourism booming, they no longer have time to do so. She rents rooms in her brand-new chalet, an occupation which keeps her busy from December to September. Antonia said that she tried for a whole year before mastering the technique of pleating the ribbon. But it was well worth her trouble: she and her mother have made over one hundred hats since they started three years ago, selling them for 280 Swiss francs (about 90 dollars) each.

Another example of this flourishing revival involves a further process in the making of the hats. Elise embroiders the hat bands for the women of Saas-Fee, Saas-Grund, and Almagell. She is fifty years old and has learned the skill from her mother, though neither of her two daughters wants to learn from her. This is their mother's sole occupation, aside from housework, and she derives great satisfaction from it. To create one of the beautiful bands Elise places the gold thread on top of the silk and fastens it to the cloth with tiny stitches of yellow silk thread. To make her embroidery look perfectly regular, she puts small pieces of cardboard in the shape of leaves or flower petals under the stitchery and cuts them away when she is finished. Black velvet or white silk is used for the band, which measures about five inches in width and two yards in length. Around the rim of it goes one-inch wide, machine-made gold lace. The finished band is fastened to the straw hat with straight pins. A rectangular piece, called *Rose*, forms the back of the hat. Finally, two silk ribbons, each one-and-a-half inches wide, are folded in bows and sewn to opposite sides of the hat. These hang decoratively on either side of the face.

The bands—and every woman is proud to have a selection of several of them—are wrapped in tissue paper and stored in a flat box during the winter. Elise estimated that the whole costume with hat would cost about 1000 Swiss francs today (about 330 dollars). Without the extra income from tourism no woman could afford to have one made. Today, almost all women wear the costume with the black-banded hat on summer Sundays, the white-banded hats

Plate 1. Painting of Mme. du Fay in mid-eighteenth-century aristocratic dress. (Heierli, 132.)

Plate 2. Frau Inalbon of Leukerbad, 1848. (Heierli, 183.)

Plate 3. Baroness of Stockalp, 1807. (Heierli, 178.)

Plate 4. Young woman of the bourgeoisie, 1820. (Heierli, 179.)

Plate 5. Girls of Saas valley, 1900. (Heierli, 160.)

Plate 6. Girl of Saas-Fee posing in native costume, 1973. (Photo by Werner Imseng.)

Plate 7. Men wearing women's hats. (Heierli, 232.)

only for the highest holidays, for baptism, and first holy communion. Though the women under forty wear only the Sunday outfits and have rejected the black costumes of the other six days, the older ones still wear them all week. Instead of the fancy hats they wear yellow scarves if their husbands are living and black scarves when they are widows.

It is important now to examine the origins of this costume, and useful documentation is found in some early paintings of the unusual hat. Plate 1 depicts Mme. du Fay wearing a mid-eighteenth-century aristocratic fashion. As a rule, today's native costumes were first worn by the nobility, and one can trace in this painting influences alive today. The full sleeves of Mme. du Fay's gold-embroidered dress and the white ruffles of the shirt sleeves are the style of the Rococo period. The white neckscarf is tucked into the *Mieder* (bodice). The small straw hat is already here; the embroidered hat band shows the same patterns as can be found today, but it is much narrower. The black ruffle around the rim, the *Kres*, is not yet present; there is black lace instead. Under the hat is a small white lace cap, which later disappeared. This picture is dated 1803, but it depicts an earlier and conservative style.

By 1807, the little cap underneath the hat was gone, but the white embroidered band was now wide enough to hide the top of the hat completely, as is shown in Plate 3. The *Kres* looks almost as if it is braided, but it might be a special way to fold the pleats. The baroness wears a short-waisted dress in the style of the empire, as does the young woman of the bourgeoisie depicted in the 1820 drawing (Plate 4); her dress, however, is much simpler, and the hat band is folded in a bow.

Plate 2 shows the evolving style of the hat as worn in the year 1848 by Frau Inalbon of Leukerbad. Her hat is very much like today's *Kreshuet*. The dress style is Biedermeier (mid-nineteenth-century style); the white scarf has become a lace collar. From this time on the wide hat band was retained. The women must have liked it, for it became the one item in the costume of the Oberwallis that was different from all the other hats worn by the women in Switzerland.

In Plate 5 are two girls from the Saas valley, their dresses in the style of the year 1900, but their hats exactly like today's. Although these were typical women's hats, we find in Plate 7 a simpler form of them, worn here by men. This group is about to leave for the alp with the livestock to spend the summer tending the cows and making cheese. Since barn work is considered in the Wallis to be women's work, the men are wearing women's hats, not for a joke, as may be seen from their grim faces, but as a regular trademark for this type of work. Today, men do not wear native costumes in the Oberwallis, but those who play in the village band wear the century-old soldiers' uniforms with high hats and plumes, handed down from their great-grandfathers. These uniforms are heirlooms of each family and are never sold.

In Plate 6 an ironic situation may be discerned. It shows a young, modern Saas-Fee girl confidently and happily wearing her native costume and posing for a picture postcard.[3] In so doing, she attracts the very tourists who fifty years ago all but destroyed native pride in traditional costume. A brief examination of any tourist center will also show that the tourist industry is using these revived traditions as an attraction to visitors through posters and printed materials of all kinds.

One final point, however, must be made. Although now seemingly interwoven with the tourist trade, this revival is not the outcome of a materialistic, moneymaking venture. The women of Saas-Fee wear their native costume because it pleases them, their husbands, their lovers, and their communities. If the last twenty years have changed these women at all, it is only in giving them confidence and a great pride in their traditional dress. They hope that with the help of the *Trachtenverein* this pride will be passed on to their daughters. They are interested in tourism solely as a means of maintaining their life style so that they can afford to have new dresses and hats made whenever they need them.

[3] Permission to reprint the photograph by Werner Imseng is gratefully acknowledged.

Negotiating Respect

Patterns of Presentation among Black Women

ROGER D. ABRAHAMS

STUDIES OF HERO TALES show how male values are embodied in narrative form. And we know (through negative evidence) how the male ideal of women is projected in such tales—chiefly with regard to inaction, constancy, and a willing subordination. But how women assert their image and values as women is seldom found in the folklore literature. We know even less about the verbal traditions of black women in particular.

However, a fairly large body of information about such sex-specific expressive capacities can be found in the autobiographical writings of black women themselves and in social scientific descriptions, a literature that tells us something about the content, if not always the devices and techniques, of black female presentations. To get at this material from a folkloristic perspective, it is necessary to analyze more conversational traditions than folklorists are generally committed to studying. Presentational devices are not unique to black women or characteristic of them but are common to all segments of the black community and as such they need to be studied to gain a fuller knowledge of what is unique to the female repertoire of presentational strategies and styles. This essay will attempt to unite the concerns of role theory and commonsense social structure as pursued by symbolic interactionists with the more usual perspectives of a performance-centered theory of folkloristics.

"Testimonies" and "Accounts" in Folkloristics

To this point, I have been using the term *presentation* for certain formulaic devices to distinguish them in some dimension from *performances*. Presentational routines are as formulaic and as subject to being learned and passed on through oral transmission as performances of traditional songs or tales, but they are not so self-consciously rendered. Rather they arise in the midst of, and as part of, the apparently spontaneous interpersonal exchanges of everyday interactions.

The kind of presentational device I focus on has been noticed in the sociological literature before. For instance, a recent study of hitchhikers develops upon the term *rap*, which the author impressionistically defines as "a purposeful reconstruction of past and present directed at explaining, enhancing and embellishing a fantasized future. This reconstruction of 'who I am' and 'where I was' in terms of 'what I will do' is an advertisement of self to significant others, with both parties aware that the presentation is, to a large extent, fantasy [i.e., fiction]."[1]

A *rap* or any other kind of presentational routine is closely related to Erving Goffman's conception of *acting out a line*. This he defines as "a pattern of verbal and nonverbal acts by which [a person] expresses his view of a situation and through this his evaluation of the participants, especially himself."[2] Acting out a line is done to assert and maintain face, "the positive social value a person claims for himself by the line others assume he has taken during a particular contact."[3] Further, "The line maintained by and for a person during contact with others tends to be of a legitimate institutionalized kind,"[4] and it is precisely the institutionalized dimension that is of interest from a folkloristic perspective, for it is just such learnable and transmittable notions of order through enactment (especially in performance) that provide an impetus for those traditional items that have been the stock in trade of our discipline.

Goffman, however, does not dwell on the formulaic and institutionalized dimension of these routines so much as the way in which their familiar order provides a means of maintaining one's image in interactional encounters and negotiations. The formulaic order in a *line*, Goffman implies, somehow induces a sense of expressive order—"an order that regulates the flow of events . . . so that anything that appears to be expressed by them will be consistent with his face."[5] Any group might then be studied both with regard to the options of *face* with which an individual is presented as part of the socialization and enculturation process and with regard to the related *lines* or *routines* available to be learned and replayed by him.

Discussing the establishment of personal and social identities in terms of such lines and routines may seem somewhat mechanical; however, the process is far from rigid for a number of reasons. Although there is a formulaic dimension to routines, each role has a number of such devices available, which may be combined for a wide range of effects. Further, there are numerous styles by which the lines may be enacted and a number of scenes in which they may be employed, each calling for modifications of strategy.

Finally, and most important, a distinction might be made between *filling* and *playing* a role. "Filling a role" would arise when there is a slot in the

[1] Abraham Miller, "On the Road: Hitchhiking on the Highway," *Society*, 10 (1973), no. 5, p. 16.

[2] "On Face Work," *Psychiatry: Journal for the Study of Interpersonal Processes*, 18 (1955), 213. Cf. "The concept of 'naming'" in Kenneth Burke, *The Philosophy of Literary Form* (New York, 1957), 1 ff., where he argues the importance of strategy and situation.

[3] Ibid., 213.

[4] Ibid., 215.

[5] Ibid., 217.

social structure, and interactions are dominated by the status relationship of the participants. There is a strong sense of the obligatory in the carrying out of such relationships; in fact, one could argue that the possibility of pursuing a line is ruled out in favor of ritualized routines that articulate and maintain decorum. "Playing a role," on the other hand, would carry a sense of optation to it. Lines become possible, and alternative approaches arise with regard to self-presentation and relationship establishment. But the presence of such options lays the individual open to the charge of "play-acting" if the role is not played successfully, or if it is successful but later proves to be inconsistent.

Lines are employed, then, primarily in relationships in which status is to be negotiated. In fact, one of the uses of the most overtly formulaic lines is to announce that one is "in play," that is, available for the type of identity negotiation most characteristic of egalitarian relationships, in which flexibility of line and spontaneity of approach are stressed.

The distinction between *filling* and *playing* roles is similar to one made by symbolic interactionists between "instrumental" and "expressive" role definition: the former arises from institutional role-assigning, the latter from a more personalistic approach. Given the egalitarian cast of American society, we have a tendency to downgrade or mask out instrumental role-taking. But, as I will argue here, Euro-Americans employ a great many more instrumental formulae in establishing family and community relationships than do Afro-Americans. Even those who most demand serious respect in the community carefully signal that they are available for role play—that the licensed dimension of playful activity may be employed as a means of negotiation with them.

There are set scenarios (often given names) in which the routines associated with the range of role formulation are situated. These events or scenes associated with role filling commonly turn on judgmental occasions, ones in which character is attacked or maintained through techniques of apology, self-assertion, or talk about others. This would include such routines as *putting up an argument, accounting for oneself, making a spiel* (or a *pitch*), *giving an excuse, gossiping, catting,* or (from black talk) *getting on someone's case.* These do not just name a type of presentation but a recurrent interactional situation and the kinds of strategies it employs. They are essentially serious, as opposed to scenes of role playing involving joking and other such licensed inversions. These other more playful routines, since they may involve greater displays of wit and even open contest, come closer to overt performances. But they are not framed and marked as performances because they involve routines that arise in conversational contexts as part of the apparently spontaneous flow of interaction and are used to assert one's perceived role, to focus or realign one's face in relation to others in the conversation and, by extension, in the narrator's network of relations. In the case of alignment, the sort of line one enacts to establish an identity with others we might call *testimony*.[6] Where interactants already know each other,

---

[6] I take the term from Lee Rainwater, *Behind Ghetto Walls* (Chicago, 1970), 284, where he mainly discusses male strategies and routines for giving testimony with regard to maturity in one's sex role.

and their need to realign this personal sense of identity arises from some disruption, we might speak of an *account*, as in "giving an account of oneself."[7]

Such presentational routines are as formulaic and repetitive as performances; we know this implicitly because when we encounter them we "know what's coming." But because they commonly arise in those more conversational contexts in which spontaneity is the norm and the formulaic is to be masked, this range of presentation is not foregrounded as it is in jokes or even anecdotes, not as intensely framed, and there are fewer markers which announce that a performance is taking place. The social fiction is maintained that not only demands the appearance of spontaneity in such talk but also signals a willingness to focus on content features to the exclusion of stylistic considerations—what we seem to mean when we say we are "just talking." To stylize is to call attention to formal and formulaic features and, thus, to make the speaker appear nonspontaneous and therefore not to be listened to or trusted in a conversationally defined situation. Though not as overtly marked, presentations are certainly as full of commonplaces and formulae as, say, jokes except that although they are preformulated and learned, they are employed in a more "open" manner, that is, in nonfixed sequences. We may therefore regard them as traditional arguments or rationalizations. These are the kinds of interactional devices that come to the folklorist's attention only when they achieve concentration and focus in such fixed-form genres as proverbs. We then recognize them as traditional because they call attention simultaneously to both the form and the content of the device.[8]

Devices of this sort will become of greater interest to folklorists as we investigate performance in everyday life, and especially the traditional presentations of women. At least with regard to black women, I have found this expanded notion of a common body of such learned devices of communication useful in understanding more fully the relationship between performance forms and styles and the social structure as perceived by members of Afro-American communities. I will consider a number of formulaic devices reported from black women's interactions and relate them to perceived Afro-American social segmentation and ways by which values (that is, ideals and norms on both the overt and covert levels) are put into action.

I do so recognizing the limitations of using reported materials that are not, for the most part, actual transcriptions of conversational exchanges. Although the language of the materials is often conversational, and thus the same formulae of argument and idea continually emerge, they are presented in auto-

---

[7] The term as used here comes from the work of Marion B. Scott and Sanford M. Lyman. See their "Accounts," *American Sociological Review*, 33 (1968), 46–62, where they define the term as "a linguistic device employed whenever an action is subjected to valuative inquiry . . . they prevent conflicts from arising by verbally bridging the gap between action and expectation" (p. 46). Michael Moerman, in his "Analysis of Lue Conversation: Providing Accounts, Finding Breaches, and Taking Sides," in David Sudnow, *Studies in Social Interaction* (New York, 1972), 75–119, utilizes the term in the sense of *accounts of*, but not *accounts for*.

[8] Alan Dundes' conception of "folk ideas" in "Folk Ideas as Units of Worldview," in *Toward New Perspectives in Folklore*, ed. Américo Paredes and Richard Bauman (Austin, Texas, 1972), 93–103, is similar to what is meant by presentation genres here.

biographical accounts in the reportorial voice and often in the past tense. In the sociological and anthropological literature, on the other hand, we are given, for the most part, distillations of reported attitudes and communication behaviors; these are even farther away from formulaic presentations. However, given the dearth of reported interactions and what I perceive to be the need to fill in the interactional portrait of the communicational life in postagrarian black communities,[9] it has seemed useful to proceed, if only to provide an outline of the recurrent scenes and settings by which black women give testimonies and accounts of their role as women. I do this recognizing that asserting one's face as a woman is, of course, only one of the types of roles (though certainly one of the most important) available to individual black women.

The essence of the negotiation involved in asserting one's role lies in a woman being both sweet and tough depending upon her capacity to define and reasonably manipulate the situation. Ideally she has the ability to *talk sweet* with her infants and peers but *talk smart* or *cold* with anyone who might threaten her self-image. She expects both good behavior and bad at all times and has routines prepared for handling and capitalizing on both. Acting and being regarded as *respectable* is not a static condition in any way; quite the contrary, the ladies most respected are often those who maintain themselves at the center of the action.

Many ethnographers of black communities have noted the importance of such routines in the assertion and maintenance of role. Ulf Hannerz, for instance, notes of the members of one neighborhood in Washington, D.C., that their opinions are often "based not only on their individual experiences but also on the interpretations their associates make for them." These interpretations are embodied in what Hannerz calls "public imagery" or "collective representations," a "motif collection into which individual experiences are fitted." Furthermore, this "culture of common sense" then provides "a screen through which impressions are sifted, as individuals become trained to take particular note of these phenomena which match or can be brought to match public images."[10]

Though Hannerz goes on to point out a few of these collective representations in the female repertoire, the great majority of his anecdotal data come from men, and this is characteristic of the ethnographic literature. Of the numerous studies we have of black life, only the studies from the Pruitt-Igoe (St. Louis) Project offer much data on female attitudes and approaches; even these deal little with the specifics of interaction, the attitudinal content being distilled from the observed conversations.[11]

Nevertheless, both males and females give a range of formulaic testimonies to values of respect and their connection with home and with the female head of the household. In this article, I will survey the ways in which respectability

---

[9] That is, communities in which cultural patterns originating in gardening cultures are maintained in the more complex and technologically oriented, sophisticated, urban social environment.

[10] *Soulside* (New York, 1969), 94.

[11] For example, see Rainwater; Joyce A. Ladner, *Tomorrow's Tomorrow: The Black Woman* (New York, 1972); see also Camille Jeffers, *Living Poor* (Ann Arbor, 1967).

is asserted and maintained in those social situations in which this norm-image is under test: while childrearing in the home; among peers; in male-female interactions. Respectability is not something a person *is*; rather it is an ideal-image that is conceived and put into action through a complex enactment of motives. Though the focus will be on strategies and directions of female presentation and maintenance of roles, the data called upon here will also cast light on those communication registers and varieties of speech regarded as situationally appropriate within the lives of black women. This suggests that further field research in this area should involve the techniques and perspectives of the ethnography of communication.

The Affirming Negations in the Opposition of the House and the Street

A problem attending the description of black presentational strategies arises from the essential differences between Euro-Americans and Afro-Americans in the systems of communication and in images of social and cultural order. These differences are especially notable in the means by which perceived oppositions are handled; in Euro-American communicational practices, we tend to minimize antagonism, to encapsulate it in "scenes," effecting closure within the scenes so that "bad feelings" are not carried away from the confrontation. Among Afro-Americans, such oppositions tend to be viewed as constant contrarieties, antagonisms that cannot be eliminated and in fact may be used to effect a larger sense of cultural affirmation of community through a dramatization of opposing forces.

We may be dealing here with a specific rendering of a cultural universal, for every culture seems to have some way of "naming" and presenting its recurrent conflicts. The very idea of drama is predicated on the process of rendering oppositions of values or allegiances playfully and interactively. Furthermore, inherent in any meaningful drama is the process Hegel saw residing in the term *aufheben*, which means at one and the same time to negate and to affirm.[12] The negation or self-cancellation occurs on the apparently temporal level, while the affirmation arises out of the embodiment and celebration of these opposing ideas or forces. It is precisely in the way a culture chooses to dramatize these oppositions that it asserts its own characteristic patterns of life style as well as art style.

This seems important to note here, because the kind of negotiation carried on by black women through their repertoire of self-presentational routines is in many ways similar to the more stylized black performances enacted by other members of the community as well. Life-affirming is carried on in such a world through an open-ended dramatization of conflicts in values and allegiances, and it is through such dramatizations that black life is invested with vigor, as well as with expressions of anxiety.

---

[12] G. W. F. Hegel, *The Phenomenology of Mind*, trans. Sir Jas. Baillie (New York, 1964), 163–164. Cf. Robert Farris Thompson, *African Art in Motion* (Los Angeles, 1974), 7–8, where he utilizes the concept to illustrate how a rhythmic beat can be suspended and maintained simultaneously as a means of aesthetic elevation.

No theme of conflict is more constant in black life than the independence and consequent opposition of the sexes. Put in its simplest terms, women are expected to be psychologically, socially, and economically independent of men. But also (and simultaneously) verbalized is an ideal of sexual interdependence, both in courtship and marriage and in the system of willingness to place oneself in the position to manipulate and be manipulated. It is precisely this simultaneous statement of independence and interdependence that results in what I will call a special Afro-American *aufheben*, that is, a unique way of affirming through the enactment of oppositions.[13] We might approach the discussion of these opposing forces through sexual dimorphism. We could express the opposition in terms of locus, through the emic contrasting of the private *home* and the public *street* worlds. Or, to put it in value terms, we could phrase it as the competition between respectability- and reputation-seeking norms. Though they are never coterminous, there is a constant sense of relationship between male values, reputation-seeking, and the public world, and between women, respectability, and the home.

However, it cannot be overstressed that black children are taught to fend for and "to go for" themselves in both the house and the street worlds, even while they are taught the value—indeed, the necessity—of cooperation. We can understand this balancing of the motives of self-reliance and cooperation quite simply by observing that black children are taught at quite an early age the entire range of housekeeping activities to assure their self-reliance in later life; but they learn to carry them out as part of the functioning cooperative unit of the household. Perhaps the point can be better made by looking at an equivalent of "going for yourself": *doing your thing*. In black talk, this does not mean acting independently of the group but rather asserting yourself *within* the group, especially in performances. Specifically, doing your thing seems to have originally meant entering into a performance by adding your voice to the ensemble, by playing off against the others, as each instrument does in jazz, for instance. A crucial part of the black aesthetic involves this voice overlap and interlock effect; everyone gets to do his own individual "thing" even while contributing to the overall sense of the whole. This, it seems to me, is the peculiar Afro-American sense of *aufheben*, the means by which opposition is transformed into affirmation. Negotiation for respectability must be viewed thus not as an attempt to sing some songs of respectability to the exclusion of alternatives, but rather as an effort to maintain a melody line against (and therefore defined by) those other voices setting up a sometimes cacophonous opposition.

By this I do not mean that there is no woman within black communities who will always assert herself in respect-seeking terms. Some will, to be sure, but these are the very ones most people will tend to regard as "uppity." The women most respected seem to be those who recognize respectability norms and decorous behaviors as negotiable. There is a good deal of legendary lore about just such women, and, in a study of stories associated with them, one of my black stu-

---

[13] Cf. Thompson, 7.

dents calls such characters "Madame Queens,"[14] describing them not only in terms of their integrity, strong will, and the sense of order they take into every encounter, but also by their need to demonstrate these qualities through dramatic interactions with those who differ, who oppose their will and sense of order.

Respectability hardly equates with the imposition of order through silence and hauteur. Firm distinctions are maintained then between being respectable and being *uppity, dicty, saddity*.[15] The former calls for maintaining self-respect through the willful imposition of order in monitoring behavior; the latter set involves setting oneself above others through a mistaken social sense that decorum is more important than vitality. And such values are embodied not only in the dramatized respectability of these ladies, but also in the many stories concerning the exploits of the most successful of these Madame Queens.

We have few studies of such exemplary stories because folkloristic interest in memorates is relatively recent. One fugitive work of J. Mason Brewer, *Aunt Dicy Tales*,[16] gives a number of representative stories concerning an older black slave who after emancipation is able to maintain her snuff-dipping habit by her willfulness and cunning, all the while proclaiming and maintaining her respectability. Similarly, Katherine L. Morgan's stories of her own family's legends concern an ancestor named Caddy, who established her integrity through the dramatizing of her values, by thumbing her nose in highly dramatic public style at those who would confront her with an insult.[17]

Such stories illustrate the flexible and highly personalistic approach to interactions characteristic of Afro-American societies in which, as noted before, the expressive or personalistic rather than the instrumental or institutional dimension of role validation is stressed. Black joke traditions underline this in portraying various hypocrisies (even to the point of satirizing grandma as being sexually wanton).[18] Though these particular stories exist primarily in the male repertoire and reflect a male perspective, the point they make is that no role automatically carries power or respect, whether preacher, old marster, or "grandma." Respect is something which must constantly be earned, negotiated.

Dramatization occurs in confrontations with those who challenge respect— with men (especially *street men* or *players*), with children, and with other women. In each social situation, set expressions and strategies indicate that the best protection against such assaults is to expect the worst. Thus, one of the most commonly encountered routines expressing the moral dominant stance of women asserts in some way that all (or most) men are untrustworthy and bad. One of Hannerz's informants notes, for instance, that "Men talk too much and

---

[14] Barbara Pyle, "Madame Queens," unpublished manuscript, 1972. Jeffers has one informant-friend whom she calls a "dowager queen," who demonstrates a similar personality. For one of the many fictional accounts of such a type, see Ernest J. Gaines, *The Autobiography of Miss Jane Pittman* (New York, 1971).

[15] For a scene in which the two are distinguished, see Rainwater, 212.

[16] Privately printed, 1956.

[17] "Caddy Buffers: Legends of a Middle Class Negro Family in Philadelphia," *Keystone Folklore Quarterly*, 11 (1966), 67–88.

[18] See my *Positively Black* (Englewood Cliffs, New Jersey, 1970), and *Deep Down in the Jungle* (Chicago, 1970), for texts.

drink too much and work too little. . . . These men always get into trouble the way they act, or they get someone else in trouble. Always something bad in their minds. Talking sweet to women, and then they don't do a thing for them when they're in trouble."[19]

Similarly, though speaking in the past tense, Ossie Guffy gives another formulation of this argument: "Lots of black people fall back on the comforting thought that the Lord will provide. To a black man, I suspect that the Lord is a black woman."[20]

This image of men is encouraged by the men themselves, so that one often finds the same accounts of misbehavior used by both sexes, but for different reasons. For instance, both women and men describe the male propensity to play around sexually as "the dog in him," that is, pure, uncontrollable animal instinct. Thus, one of Hannerz' female informants notes, "Sure they're all sweet to start with, and you have a good time together, but then they start running around with another woman the moment you turn your back. You hear people say every man has a dog in him? That ain't no joke you know."[21] Another discussion between men invokes the same argument, but this time as an excuse: "Men have a little bit of dog in them, you know. That's why they can't leave the women alone."[22]

Men have a great deal to do with maintaining the image of female respectability, even when they regard actual respect-seeking behavior as insincere or hypocritical. They support the image for a number of reasons: to maintain a good environment for raising their children; to maintain a locus which continues to represent a life-style alternative that can be turned to if and when they choose to give up their reputation-seeking ways; to provide a given model of behavior that can be depended upon when a man wants to manipulate a woman. But with regard to this last ploy, just as men evince their badness in order to enhance their reputation, women will define the strength and force of their respectability by successfully contending against such men.

The locus of respectability is the home; the operation of the household is both the real and the symbolic means by which these overt social values are put into practice. But black talk commonly recognizes that this private sphere of activity will be under constant attack from the more public "street" world and that it is in the inevitable confrontation between these worlds that a female is able to enact being a woman.

In a marvelous piece of portraiture, Maya Angelou describes her mother in her autobiography *I Know Why the Caged Bird Sings*. After discussing how her mother maintained herself financially as a public character, she notes that, in spite of her mother's availability for rough joking from other street-people,

---

[19] Hannerz, 97. He discusses this range of argument extensively, 95–102. For similarly stereotypical account and testimony behavior from men, see my *Positively Black*, 109, 112.

[20] Caryle Ladner and Ossie Guffy, *Ossie: The Autobiography of a Black Woman* (New York, 1972), 3. See also Jeffers, 35.

[21] Hannerz, 97; see also Jeffers, 35, 50, where she notes the recurrence of this theme in women's talk.

[22] Hannerz, 99.

"everyone knew that although she cussed freely as she laughed, no one cussed around her, and certainly no one cussed her."[23] This set of distinctions demonstrates one of the problems encountered by black women whenever they must go into a public situation, for some attempt will commonly be made by them to balance the need to present themselves as successful public interactants with the need to maintain the sense of female respectability that is the ideal of feminine "face" in the community. As Beverly Stoeltje's informant "Evelyn" analyzes it (in another recent study), there is an important behavioral distinction between acting *at home* and *on the street*, a distinction that goes beyond the places where interactions take place to the style by which exchanges are carried out.

The "lady on the street" is . . . they could call it a pick-up lady. She is on the street, man after man, day after day. Just as I get up and go to the job, she gets up and goes to the street.

But you take a lady *at home* that goes out, very seldom would accept a drink from a man outside. If they buy you a drink, they think you are sittin' waiting for a pick-up. But if a lady go out by herself and sit in a particular place, she's looking for a pickup and she consider herself a lady on the street.

The lady is *at home* is a very independent lady. She leaves home, . . . knowing where her kids is, and knowing that 12:30 or 1:00 o'clock it's nice to come home . . . knowing that everything was taken care of at home. . . . The lady on the street . . . she leaves home with nothing and it's nothing at home either. . . . Nine chances out of ten they give the kids up, or they don't even have time, they leave 'em at a baby sitter's on Thursday night and don't see 'em until the next Thursday. The lady at home knows she have to go home at a certain hour to even respect her kids, draggin' in and out at all times of the night. And a lady on the street will bring 'em in to her apartment, where a lady at home respect her household. . . .[24]

Thus, at least for this one informant, being *at home* does not mean staying at home but maintaining the integrity of the household in the face of possible incursions from the street; her respect for the home begets respect from the others in it but must be asserted in many nonhome situations.[25]

This dichotomy between house and street is certainly far from unique to black communities; as in other groups, the basic distinction is between private and public realms and their associated behaviors. Also not uncommonly, the two worlds become identified to some extent with the age and sex of their citizens, the household world being associated with the very young, the old, and with women, the street with adolescents and young adults and primarily with men. Herbert Gans describes much the same complex as a lower-class phenomenon

[23] New York, 1971, 176.

[24] Beverly Stoeltje, "Bow-Legged Bastard: A Manner of Speaking," in *Folklore Annual of the University Folklore Association*, Nos. 4–5, ed. Tom Ireland, Joanne Krauss, Beverly Stoeltje, Frances Terry (Austin, Texas, 1972–1973), 174. See the similar argument pursued by a Mississippi country informant in George Mitchell's *Blow My Blues Away* (Baton Rouge, 1971), 23.

[25] See my "Black Talking on the Streets," in *Explorations in the Ethnography of Speaking*, ed. Richard Bauman and Joel Sherzer (Cambridge and New York, 1974), 534.

in a study of working class Italian-Americans.[26] It is not this distinction of worlds that is distinctively black, then, but the types and styles of interactions carried on within and between the denizens of the two domains. Blacks regard different styles of communication behaviors as appropriate to these two worlds.

The most important distinction between the household and the street world turns on the roles and the role types available in the two realms. In the home one's role is generally determined by family relationships. Roles are assigned according to where one stands vis-à-vis the distribution of power and responsibility within the household. Generally, even with a resident paterfamilias, in the Afro-American family it is *Momma* who delegates responsibilities, because her respectability is judged by how effectively her household is run. She must both encounter, and guard her private world from, the incursions of the more public streets, incursions that constantly threaten from many sides. In this, her values on being *treated respectably* come into conflict all too often with the values of those in the street life, whose names depend on reputation rather than respectability.[27] *Maintaining a rep*, and especially a *high rep*, means acting with a display style and spending one's resources in a manner that threatens Momma in many ways.

Momma is not the only one who is basically ambivalent about the street and its public life. From the perspective of Momma and her values, everything on the street provides a threat to her respectability; any kind of rudeness, excessive noise, or playing may be viewed by her as an attack. But to many, and especially the young men and women, the street world (which includes other public places) is *where the action is* and where one is expected to have fun. Though men find it easier to handle street situations, even they must be wary at all times of the threats coming from such a world. On the street, one is constantly in danger of being *hustled*, of having a *game run* on him. Anyone who goes public (especially in the cities) is open to such *trickification*.

> You know yourself, man, when you walk out in the streets you have to be ready. Everybody walking out there is game on everybody else. If you don't watch what you're doing, before you know it you're going to be put in a trick bag. . . . It's true where the members are found [i.e., wherever Blacks are congregating]. Our people are always plotting and scheming.[28]

This kind of account could be given by male or female. In this specific case, it was uttered by a man threatened by the street not so much for himself but for his wife, whom he felt had been sheltered from the tricks and thus had been easily taken in. (This is one example of why and how men attempt to maintain the respect image for women.) He goes on to argue that for a man, it is easy

---

[26] *The Urban Villagers* (New York, 1962).

[27] Peter Wilson, "Reputation and Respectability: Suggestions for Caribbean Ethnology," *Man*, 4 (1969), 70–84. See also my "Black Talking on the Streets"; *Positively Black*; and "Joking: The Training of the Man of Words in Talking Broad," in *Rappin' and Stylin' Out*, ed. Thomas Kochman (Champaign-Urbana, Illinois, 1972).

[28] Rainwater, 21.

to adopt the street attitude of "Do unto others before they do unto you,"[29] but for a woman it is more difficult, and she can lose her *name* as a result.

I have heard reports that my wife is running around . . . it really does hurt me because I wonder how she could have time to be a mother and a player at the same time. . . . It is impossible for a woman to take care of her child and be out in the streets at the same time. . . . *I would rather have us fighting and fussing all the time and have her with me than to have her get a bad name by being out on the streets.*[30]

Such arguments are so familiar and formulaic that they begin to seem almost proverbial (although lacking the conciseness of form). Perhaps because of the very repetitive nature of such arguments they are seldom reported with fidelity to the situation and to progression of a communicative interaction. But values and life-style alternatives are learned and celebrated more through such routines and the commonplaces of their argument than through formal stories.

Negotiating at Home with Children

Being a mother does not make one a *Momma*, even when one begins to set up a household of one's own. The role must be acted upon appropriately or the rest of the community will not recognize a woman in that role. If a woman maintains her family connections, she must continue to respect her Momma, and that means acting appropriately when in her own home as well as in her Momma's. Otherwise her Momma may be accused of raising her children improperly (though she may argue in her own defense that she can't control what happens outside her own home). Just how this operates is explained by one of Carol Stack's informants in discussing her first baby, which she had at nineteen.

I was really wild in those days, out on the town all hours of the night, and every night and weekend I layed my girl on my mother. I wasn't living home at the time, but mama kept Christine most of the time. One day mama up and said I was making a fool of her and she was going to take my child and raise her right. She said I was immature and had no business being a mother the way I was acting. All my mama's people agreed and there was nothing I could do. So mama took my child.[31]

This records both an attitude and a commonly encountered routine on the part of Momma or some other lady presenting herself as respectable, in distinction to a younger woman too much on the streets. As one Momma in a parallel situation put it succinctly, "I'm not gonna have those babies out in the street. They're gonna stay here even if [their mother] moves out. I'll not have it, not knowing who's taking care of them."[32] Again, what is a fixed account in the repertoire of one person (the young mother) becomes both a testimony and a different sort of account in the presentation of another. But they both reflect the same ideal and public image.

Respectability is expressed not only in such testimonies but also in the strategies and styles of communication insisted upon as appropriate in the house

[29] Ibid., 22.
[30] Ibid., 29. Italics in the original. For a similar routine from a woman, see Jeffers, 43.
[31] "Parenthood and Personal Kinship Networks among Blacks on Aid," unpublished manuscript.
[32] Rainwater, 205.

or some other place regarded as respectable, such as church or even lodge. One of the routines of respectability involves monitoring others' presentational techniques. In general, women are expected to be more restrained than men in their talk, less loud, less public, and much less abandoned. They speak in a register closer to standard conversational English than do the men. Girls are lectured by both Daddy and Momma on never talking loudly or cursing, not even when involved in street encounters. As Louise Meriwhether explained it: "Daddy didn't even want me to say darn. He was always telling me: 'It's darn today, damn tomorrow, and next week it'll be goddamn. You're going to grow up to be a lady, and ladies don't curse.' "[33] Any kind of public talk may not be respectably ladylike to a man. Zora Neale Hurston has one of her male characters note of his wife when someone asks her during a public occasion to give a speech: "mah wife don't know nothin' 'bout no speechmaking. Ah never married her for nothin' lak dat. She's uh woman and her place is in de home." (But the novel relates how a lady learns to speak in the development of her self-respect.)[34]

The house as the locus of a woman's sense of respectability causes Momma to monitor constantly her own as well as others' talk there. Silence is also highly valued in children (especially in the presence of Momma). What Virginia Heyer Young notes of mother-toddler interactions is by other accounts characteristic of mother-child communications in general. At the point of changing from infant (*lap-baby*) to toddler (*knee-baby*), a perceptible shift occurs, in which, among other things, the speaking variety seems to be altered, and "Children speak less to adults and get along adequately with 'Yes'm' and 'No'm.' "[35]

Within the home the child is expected to observe and, in learning tasks, to emulate the maternal figure. This means that whenever Momma is present, a child will watch what she does and observe her reactions. He will test her constantly but also will expect to be reprimanded by the strong glance, by the direct question concerning his actions, or by admonitions.

In this ambience words between adults and children are extremely restricted; few words are used, and tasks are broken down into small units "with brief directions for each short task following on the completion of the previous one."[36] In the situation in which the mother's respectability is constantly felt to be tested, any repeated communication—verbal or otherwise—is loaded with significance. Mother's words are highly weighted in such a system, giving her directive power with an economy of means.

That is not to say that there is no interaction between mother and child, only that interactions are nonreciprocal. Imperatives are given, informational ques-

[33] *My Daddy Was a Numbers Runner* (New York, 1969), 28.

[34] *Their Eyes Were Watching God* (New York, 1969), 39.

[35] "Family and Childhood in a Southern Negro Community," *American Anthropologist*, 72 (1970), 282. For data that argue somewhat in the same direction, but are not read in this manner, see Jeffers, 60 ff. Her remarks on "independence training" at this stage are apposite, if sometimes inconsistent.

[36] Young, 286. Young's observations of parent-child interactions are paralleled in many regards in Martha Coonfield Ward, *Them Children: A Study in Language Learning* (New York, 1971), 36–38, 71–73.

tions asked, but seldom is either used to instigate verbal communication so much as to produce action on the part of the child. This means, among other things, that "Parents are not in the habit of asking questions to which they already know the answer . . . neither do [they] indulge in pleasantries."[37]

The value placed on silence in the home (on the part of children) is one facet of an elaborate ideal of deference, which includes learning proper modes of address, how and when to act in the presence of adults, and how and where to look (mutely) when being addressed by an older person.[38] Thus, one of the most important routines by which a woman defines her respectable sex-role is by speaking little with the mouth and a great deal with the eyes, the arms and shoulders, the whole set of the body.

Neither Momma (nor other adults) will be expected always to behave in accord with their own ideals in talking style or in actions. One has the feeling, from discussions with a wide range of black people and from perusing the literature, that consonance between actual and ideal behavior was and is greater in country and small-town black life than in the cities—in spite of jokes to the contrary. But this may be an operation of our very American pastoral sympathies, our desire to maintain an image of our agrarian past as a time when we lived more harmoniously, more in tune with both nature and our social ideals. In any case, the child observes early and often that there are at least two standards of behavior in front of Momma, one for children and one for adults; though their own noise is despised, the environment is filled with other noises, against which they learn to play. Further, numerous kinds of aggressive verbal behaviors go on in front of Momma, and in fact Momma engages in them. These behaviors are denied children, at least until they attain young adult status—and even then they will probably have to fight for the right.

To this point in this section I have focused on the respect routines between Momma and children. But a strong countervalent tendency is noted in the literature: children are encouraged from the earliest age to be aggressive, even hostile, to Momma. This encouragement is related to the standard maternal account for any kind of misbehavior, namely that children are often "born bad," with all the ambiguous meaning of *badness* in black talk.[39]

For instance, children are encouraged to fight back if they learn how to do so properly, by acting linguistically as adults. Ward points out that "while children may be punished for crying and making too much noise, they are not responsible for what might be thought of as 'linguistic offenses,' sassiness, for example. A child who adopts the same tone and phrases as his mother will be laughed at . . . a child's cursing or profanity [too] is interpreted as funny."[40]

Indeed, this kind of competitive spirit between parents and children in which the child shows an adult ability (even to the point of hitting his mother) is in many cases applauded, in spite of the obvious challenge to authority and re-

[37] Ward, 72–73.
[38] Maya Angelou describes this behavior ideal in her reminiscences of her childhood in Stamps, Arkansas, in *I Know Why*, 22–23.
[39] See, for instance, the brief discussion in Jeffers, 65, 67.
[40] Ward, 68.

spectability. This acting like an adult is one of the features characteristic of the highly approved role of *little mama* or *nurse mama* but is also a motive with boys.[41] The approval stems from the ambivalence toward acting bad, meaning not only to act disrespectfully but to do so by displaying self-reliance.

However, children hear not only that all children are bad, but that so are all men, and so are all women. Young girls, as they are taught their household work-skills, are also taught that they had better learn them well because chances are they are going to have to run households on their own since men cannot be trusted to do their share or to stay in one place very long. And young boys are given the same argument about girls as the reason for them to learn the entire range of household maintenance tasks. This encourages children to learn and practice these tasks well, and thus enables Momma to maintain her sense of respectability. But it also teaches children that the only kind of relationship, indeed the only kind of love, on which one can depend is that of Momma for her children.

Saying that one expects the doings of all of these others to be *bad* is, then, among other things to evaluate from the perspective of the house and its leader. Whether this means that there is a real expectation of badness on the part of all others is hardly important (if it could be ascertained). In this Afro-American perspective, the overt explanation of bad behavior will be something like, "Well that's the way men (or women or children or even Negroes) are." Rather than masking alternative (perhaps deviant) behaviors, the black approach seems to be to expect anything and to develop techniques for capitalizing on the good and perhaps the bad as well. Whatever the causes for this pattern of expectation, one effect is that among blacks action (and talk) is constantly being judged, and generally from the perspective of respectability values. This makes it all the more important that Momma's household stand up well under scrutiny, lest she receive the ill judgment of her peers and community.

One of the components of this argument is that not only order but also work become identified with home and Momma, play and action with the streets. Such associations are important for a number of reasons, not least of which is that when one of her children is working outside the home it should be in part to help Momma with the bills. This obligation (as many have noted) operates as a norm throughout one's life and supplies men with one of their consistent routines of making a bow toward respectability values. For instance, Friedland and Nelkin note in their study of the culture of black migratory laborers:

People believe that, regardless of how little money one earns, one must financially support "mother." They may disrespect their wives and women, but mothers seem sacrosanct. George sends his mother $20.00 every week. He says his mother is much more important to him than his fiancée because "you can have lots of wives but you only have one mother. . . ." James said even though he couldn't stand his mother, he sent her $20.00 every week. "My mother was the one who brought me into this world and I owe her for it."[42]

---

[41] See Jeffers, 64, and Ladner, 60 ff., for descriptions of this role and the social situation in which it operates. See especially "The Case of Kin," Ladner, 65–67.

[42] Friedland and Nelkin, *Migrant* (New York, 1972), 124–125.

Negotiating with Men

Giving money is one important way a man shows his respect for a woman, particularly one who is taking care of his children, whether she is Momma, or his *old lady*, or his wife. This is especially so because the contrary pull faced by many men is the need to maintain their male friendship networks and develop a good reputation.[43] In a situation of scarce resources, the willingness to respect a woman and her household needs becomes a matter of being able to attain the basic necessities. Certainly, then, one of the central requirements for asserting respectability is the ability to maintain the household as a home.[44] Unfortunately, almost nothing in the literature concerns the interactions of men and women already in a household-keeping kind of arrangement. What we do have reported are those areas surveyed above in which women discuss the generic failures of men—and one can assume that many of the same formulaic arguments arise (though from different perspectives) in arguments with a husband or "old man."

Such problems are part of a larger man-woman contest that is carried on both in the home and in more public settings. With younger girls, contact with males is a very deep part of their definition of themselves as maturing women. In her study of black adolescent females, Joyce Ladner notes: "Girls realize early that one of the ways to achieve the status of a woman is to learn the more complex game that is involved in male-female relationships. There are appropriate things to say and ways to behave at appropriate times in the interchange of communication and contact."[45] Furthermore, it is through relationships with men that girls achieve womanhood status not only in men's eyes, but in the eyes of their own peers and of adults generally as well.

With regard to how maturing girls operate in male-female situations, Ladner points out two general types: those who are "childish," sincere and innocent, and the more sophisticated type, who "rather frequently engage . . . in manipulative strategies . . . [who] had learned the rules of the game and devised [their] own strategies. . . ."[46] Both types depend upon the female making herself available for public interactions with men. The naïve type would then be so defined by an essentially *sweet-talking* approach on the part of the man, with a minimum of vocal response on the woman's part. The sophisticate, on the other hand, asserts her self-sufficiency through an answering style, one which relies on joking *smart talk* to assert distance and make room for her own manipulation.

These alternatives seem to have operated for some time in Afro-American communities in the United States, as can be observed in the southern court-

---

[43] See Peter Wilson; Hannerz; and Elliot Liebow, *Tally's Corner* (Boston, 1967), *passim*.

[44] See Jeffers' description (pp. 37–41) of the Queene family problems arising from a husband's buying a car and running around in it.

[45] Ladner, 180.

[46] Ibid., 182. Unfortunately, for our present purposes, Ladner's data are derived from highly directed interviews; thus we are given little information on what these strategies are and how they operate.

ship scenes found in fictional renderings; Alston Anderson describes one, a sweet-talking procedure:

One day I was standing outside the barbershop with some of the boys. Miss Florence come by on her way home from the schoolhouse, and they got to signifying:

"Mmmmmmm-*mph*! What a fine day *this* is!"

"Yes, Lawd, it sho is."

"My, my, what a *purty* day!"

"How do, Miss Florence!"

"How do you do."

"Yes Lawd, I'd sleep in the streets fawdy days and fawdy nights for a day like *that*!"

"Y'all hush your signifying," I said. "That there's a *lady*, and I won't have y'all signifying 'bout her like that."

I said it in a tone of voice that wasn't loud, but I knew she heard it. Next time I seen her she had a nice little smile for me, but I acted like nothing had ever happened.[47]

Courtship patterns in the South were primarily characterized by males adopting the eloquent "fancy talk" variety of speaking as a means of paying respect, discoursing in a code replete with latinate words and an appropriately expansive style of delivery.[48] This style of talking was commonly employed by men and by the young of both sexes whenever they were in a place, like church or school, which was regarded by the community as one in which proper (that is, ideal household) behaviors were appropriate. But it is also found in totally male groups as one register in which a man-of-words may *run the changes*, demonstrating his verbal abilities.[49] Puckett, reviewing the literature on courtship, noted that "the suitor with a retinue of grandiose words had a decided advantage, and many plantations had an old slave experienced in the words and ways of courtship to instruct young gallants in the way in which they should go in the delicate matter of winning the girl of their choice."[50] He provides us with a number of examples of the kinds of speeches to use on such occasions.

This was not the only approach to such male-female talking-relationships in the South, however. Equally characteristic seems to have been the bantering street encounter such as the acting-out courtships reported by Hurston in a number of her works, in which eloquence becomes mixed with tomfoolery and *smart talk*:

... here comes Bootsie, and Teadi and Big 'oman down the street making out they are pretty by the way they walk. They have got that fresh, new taste about them like young mustard greens in the spring, and the young men on the porch are just bound to tell them about it and buy them some treats.

"Heah come mah order right now," Charlie Jones announces and scrambles off the porch to meet them. But he has plenty of competition. A pushing, shoving show of

[47] *Lover Man* (New York, 1959).

[48] Joe L. Dillard, *Black English* (New York, 1972).

[49] Hurston, *Their Eyes*, 37–38, and *Jonah's Gourd Vine* (Philadelphia, 1939), 70–72. The latter has commentary on how not to make such speeches.

[50] Puckett, 29–30.

gallantry. They all beg the girls to just buy anything they can think of. Please let them pay for it. Joe is begged to wrap up all the candy in the store and order more. All the peanuts and soda water—everything!

"Gal, Ah'm crazy 'bout you," Charlie goes on to the entertainment of everybody. "Ah'll do anything in the world except work for you and give you mah money."

The girls and everybody else help laugh. They know it's not courtship. It's acting-out courtship and everybody is in the play.[51]

The scene proceeds with further mock-courtship in which the men vie, in elevated hyperbole, over who will get the hand of one of the girls, Daisy. It ends on this note:

"Daisy, Ah'll take uh job cleanin' out de Atlantic Ocean fuh you any time you say you so desire." There was a great laugh and then they hushed to listen.

"Daisy," Jim began, "You know mah heart and all de ranges uh mah mind. And you know if Ah wuz ridin' up in uh earoplane way up in de sky and Ah looked down and seen you walkin' and knowed you'd have tuh walk ten miles tuh git home, Ah'd step backward offa dat earoplane just to walk home wid you."[52]

If a woman places herself in a public situation, she is in jeopardy of having to contend with men and their *jive* (or to use the southern term, *high pro*). What is a serious variety of communication in the enclosed settings of home or church becomes a playful one in the more open context of porch and road and country store. If a woman's sense of respectability is challenged in such a situation, she may fight fire with fire, becoming as verbally open and aggressive as her contenders, resorting to a very tendentious sort of *smart talking*. Hurston again provides us with a description of such a scene, which begins with a man seriously kidding the heroine, Janie, as she waits on him in a store.

"I god almighty! A woman stay round uh store till she get old as Methusalem and still can't cut a little thing like a plug of tobacco! Don't stand dere rollin' yo' pop eyes at me wid yo' rump hangin' nearly to you' knees!"

"Nah, Ah ain't no young gal no mo' but den Ah ain't no old woman neither. Ah reckon Ah looks mah age too. But Ah'm uh woman every inch of me, and Ah knows it. Dat's uh whole lot more'n *you* kin say. You big-bellies round here and put out a lot of brag, but 'tain't nothin' to it but yo' big voice. Humph! Talkin' 'bout *me* lookin' old! When you pull down yo' britches, you look lak de change uh life."[53]

Elevated "fancy talking" has not been totally lost in the flight from the South, but it becomes mixed in with other varieties, as one way in which a young man may *run the changes* while *rapping* to a woman. For instance, Claudia Mitchell-Kernan reports a conversation she had with some young men in a park, in which talking fancy talk and talking smart are resorted to by both man and woman (in this case the author herself).

I: Baby, you a real scholar. I can tell you want to learn. Now if you'll just cooperate a li'l bit, I'll show you what a good teacher I am. But first we got to get into my area of expertise.

---

[51] Hurston, *Their Eyes*, 58–59.
[52] Ibid., 60. See also Hurston, *Mules and Men* (Philadelphia, 1935), 90–91.
[53] Hurston, *Their Eyes*, 68–69.

R: I may be wrong but seems to me we already in your area of expertise.

I: You ain' so bad yourself, girl. I ain't heard you stutter yet. You a li'l fixated on your subject though. I want to help a sweet thang like you all I can. I figure all that book learning you got must mean you been neglecting other areas of your education.

II: Talk that talk! . . .

R: Why don't you let me point out where I can best use your help.

I: Are you sure you in the best position to know?

(laughter)

I: I'mo leave you alone, girl. Ask me what you want to know. Tempus fugit, baby.[54]

This fashion of interaction that includes talking smart is just one of a number of black types of speaking which involve an agonistic motive and the use of cleverness. Smartness may be found in the repertoires of men, women, and children, but it does seem to be especially important in women's talk both with each other and with men. Furthermore, it seems to arise as a means of marking a serious (or potentially serious) personal antagonism, thus distinguishing it from the overtly playful yet often agonistic *talkin' shit* or *woofin'*.[55]

"Talking smart" routines develop in male-female interactions in a range of situations—from the totally public badinage in which the interactants entertain on-lookers while they establish joking as the basis of their relationship to the dyadic interaction between two already deeply involved participants in which the smart talk is intended to produce strategic advantage (and thus to modify the behavior of the man). Strong women develop reputations for their talking ability. As Maya Angelou reports it, her mother was one of these.

The good Lord gave her a mind and she intended to use it to support her mother and her children. She didn't need to add "And have a little fun along the way."

In the street the people were genuinely happy to see her. "Hey, baby, what's the news?"

"Everything's steady, baby, steady."

"I can't win, 'cause of the shape I'm in." (Said with a laugh that belied the content.)

"You all right, momma?"

"Aw, they tell me the whitefolks still in the lead." (Said as if that was not quite the whole truth.) . . .

With all her jollity, Vivian Baxter [her mother] had no mercy. There was a saying in Oakland at the time which, if she didn't say it herself, explained her attitude. The saying was, "Sympathy is next to shit in the dictionary, and I can't even read." Her temper was not diminished with the passing of time, and when a passionate nature is not eased with moments of compassion, melodrama is likely to take the stage.[56]

[54] Mitchell-Kernan, *Language Behavior in a Black Urban Community*, Monographs of the Language Behavior Laboratory, University of California, Berkeley, No. 2 (February, 1971), 106–107.

[55] Stoeltje's informant makes such a distinction though on somewhat different grounds (pp. 164 ff.). For a discussion of the range of street-talking types, see my "Black Talking on the Streets," in Bauman and Sherzer, eds., *Explorations*.

[56] Angelou, 174–176.

The message is clear: if you have anything to do with such a woman, especially as a man, don't expect to be able to beat her at the talking game, at *signifying*. Thus, smartness becomes one way of maintaining distance and demonstrating the kind of *cool* that contributes to respect behavior. With the data provided by Mitchell-Kernan and Stoeltje, and from the fiction of Zora Neale Hurston and more recently Toni Cade Bambara,[57] one gets the impression that there is a different style and strategy of female signifying in which personal reproach is put into impersonal attack form. Mitchell-Kernan, in her discussion of *signifying*, provides most of her examples from woman-humor, and they are of this less immediately personal and aggressive sort. For instance, she reports a conversation between a husband and wife:

Wife: Where are you going?
Husband: I'm going to work.
Wife: . . . a suit, tie and white shirt. You didn't tell me you got a promotion.[58]

Talking Sweet and Smart to Each Other

The female style of signifying is, of course, not restricted to male-female encounters but may be employed in any situation of competition or conflict in which women find themselves. Nowhere does the available data seem less satisfactory than in the area of women talking smart among themselves, as a kind of female equivalent of "talking shit." Fiction by black women writers like Hurston and Bambara strongly suggests that the same devices of talking smart are used, but more playfully, in some peer-group interactions. See especially the latter's tour de force short story, "The Johnson Girls."[59] There is a difference of tone between these depictions and those describing similar rapping among black men, but without much more observational data it is not possible to detail what this difference is—other than the frequency of indirect and metaphoric phrasing and a less prolonged agonistic tone (that is, the contest elements seem to last for a shorter duration in women's talk). Also, additional data are needed to judge what importance such interactions have in the maintenance of the respect dimension of being female.

What we do know is that discussion of each other's behavior does go on between and among women, in front of each other and otherwise, and that such talk provides a running commentary on how individuals adhere to respect ideals or depart from them. Not all such talk is demeaning. As Hannerz depicts the situation, women are threatened when one of their number dramatizes herself as departing from the norms of respectability. "It is the women who complain most frequently about the disorderliness of specific individuals or of their neighborhood in general."[60] To do so is to give testimonial to their adherence to the respectable female role expectations. This is a kind of "gossiping" household performance that keeps "the public imagery of the 'good woman' going by speaking favorably about female behavior and morals more often than not,

---

[57] See especially her short stories, collected as *Gorilla, My Love* (New York, 1972).
[58] Mitchell-Kernan, 180.
[59] Bambara, 144–159.
[60] Hannerz, 96.

and by finding excuses for female infractions of mainstream behavior when confronted with evidence more often than they do for men."[61] Gossiping, then, does not just mean *bad-mouthing*. Women talking about the business of other women comment both approvingly and disapprovingly, all the while creating the impression of constant surveillance of behavior.

There is some question about the register and style in which such talking is carried out. Age and situational factors are important, but under certain circumstances the women may use a different register of speaking than is found in their communication with men or children. Hannerz describes these "sociable conversations" between women when they are commenting favorably about each other as being carried on in a "tone of relaxed sweetness, sometimes bordering on the saccharine, which contrasts sharply with the heated arguments of the male peer group."[62] This may be so when sweet talking among women occurs in the house; the arguments and discussions of men are carried out in the more public arena of the street world, where *playing* and *loud-talking*—"talk loud and draw a crowd"—may provide a reputation-maintaining device.

The ones most threatened by gossip are, of course, those who are heads of households, and they go to some lengths to maintain their names; name, in such circumstances, extends to a woman's house, which includes her man, and her children, insofar as their doings relate to the maintenance of the household. Just where the line is drawn is often a fine problem, as this conversation reported by Hylan Lewis from a Piedmont black community indicates. Lewis' informant is discussing her daughter's illegitimate children and the gossip excited by them:

I had to lay Miss A— out about talking about my daughter and her three babies. I told her that although she had got them babies, that not nary one was got in my house; she got them away from my house; nobody, I mean nobody, can accuse me of letting some man lie up in my house with my daughter. . . . *I keeps my house decent.* What they does outside, I can't help that. I'm going to take care of them as long as I is able.[63]

A woman, then, has to be cognizant of the fact that her behavior is going to be discussed, especially with regard to how she keeps her household under control.[64] On the other hand, this same gossip network accords her vocal acclaim in the behaviors they judge to be appropriate.

Furthermore, a woman does not have to abide by the judgment of the network. She may simply ignore such pressures, especially if she has made the decision to be on the streets, *playing*. Or she may continue to behave as she deems right but to provide accounts for her behavior in a court that generally allows a good deal of latitude if these accounts are indeed forthcoming. Or she may adopt an in-between position, giving an account to one member of the network with whom she feels most secure. In extreme situations, she may dramatically give

---

61 Ibid.
62 Ibid.
63 *Blackways of Kent* (New Haven, 1964), 104.
64 See, for instance, the remarks in Jeffers, 69, concerning how children are dressed; also the discussion in Ann Moody's *Coming of Age in Mississippi* (New York, 1968), 69 ff., on how the specter of being bad-mouthed by a Madam Queen operated in gaining converts to a local church in a small-town situation.

counter testimony or a justifying account of ultimate respectability to a person who has chosen to use supposed misbehavior in her own testimony for respect.[65]

Numerous means of defense against gossip may not only argue back but propose alternative interpretations of what is meant by behaving respectably and what therefore leads to being accorded respectability by the community or by some of its members.[66] Though "Mouth-Almighties" exist, they are not just malicious gossipers; they provide a means of dramatizing one dimension of behavior in the dynamic of the black cultural system. They are purveyors of "words walking without masters"[67] but in a fuller sense than Hurston seems to have meant by that phrase. The words are those of community and of traditional image, and if they sometimes hurt they also act as part of a communication system that has maintained a sense of community in some trying times.

Respectability and Black Culture

I have been discussing the feasibility of studying social structure through learned interaction patterns that exist both on the level of role relationships and on that of style and the formularized content of communications. These are "learned" in the sense that individuals draw upon formulaic routines as a means of typing themselves and others. In this way I hoped to establish for women the same kind of continuities between talking styles and ascribed role and status as I have attempted in previous descriptions of self-dramatizations of black men. Here, however, the subject has to some degree resisted such a performance-centered folkloristic perspective, for we have so very few data concerning the communication and performance habits of women. We know something of the importance of women being able to answer a rap with a rap and to maintain self-respect through a control over the speaking going on in their presence through such means as smart talk and maintaining silence.

Clearly, respectability is an important role feature to negotiate as a woman matures. Because respect is equated in certain situations with money and attention to family maintenance, this negotiation may be carried on as a necessity of life. Looking at it from the larger performance perspective, negotiations are clearly also an important way in which some of the crucial dimensions of the contrarieties of black culture are asserted and maintained. Respect is never simply an attitude that brings about a monitoring of behavior in the presence of a respectable woman; it is also an ideal susceptible to being tested and the source of an important, and often entertaining, drama, which invests black life with its constant sense of adaptability, endurance, and vitality.

In looking at the amazing history of how Afro-Americans have been able to endure and proliferate in the alien New World, we must never underestimate the role of respectability and women. It was not just as "Mammy" that black women persisted in asserting their self-respect. The "Mammy" role grew in

---

[65] For examples of both these last two strategies, see the opening of Hurston, *Their Eyes*.

[66] In a sense, this is the theme of such diverse works as Hurston's *Their Eyes*, and Lorraine Hansberry's *Raisin in the Sun*, both of which survey some of the possibilities of achieving and maintaining respect, at different places and in different historical times.

[67] Hurston, *Their Eyes*, 3.

importance because of the manipulation by which respect might be negotiated even in the enslavement situation. The record on this is clear. Henry Breen's statement about St. Lucian blacks from the perspective of the plantation owner in 1844 is characteristic of plantation literature on this issue: "in the Negro's ear, . . . to be deemed *insolent* is the lowest depth of degradation, [but] to be held *respectable* is the highest step in the ladder of social distinctions. From Marigot to Maborya, from Cape Maynard to the Mole-à-chiques, respectability is the aim and end of every pursuit."[68]

Respectability never provides the only set of possible actions, but it does set out alternatives, which must be borne in mind in making any assessment of the systems and dramatizations of black culture. Though "acting respectable" means filling a role of woman and especially of Momma as demanded by the social structure, the more one looks at the negotiations the more one sees that the role is also *played* in most situations, and often joyously.[69]

[68] Henry J. Breen, *A History of St. Lucia* (London, 1844), 200–201.
[69] Some of these ideas were embodied in earlier papers: "A True and Exact Survey of Talking Black," read at the Conference on the Ethnography of Communication, Austin, Texas, April 21–23, 1972, sponsored by the Social Science Research Council's Committee on Sociolinguistics, and "Toward a Black Rhetoric," prepared for the Conference on Black Communications, University of Pittsburgh, Pittsburgh, Pennsylvania, November, 1972, sponsored by the American Speech Communications Association. I wrote the present paper while on a grant from the Center for Urban Ethnography. I am indebted to my wife, Barbara, for her suggestions for revision, and to many of my students, especially Barbara Pyle, Minta Tidwell, Beverly Stoeltje, Danielle Roemer, and Claire Farrer, editor of this issue, for their commentary.

The **Bormliza**

Maltese Folksong Style and Women*

NORMA McLEOD
MARCIA HERNDON

IN THE MEDITERRANEAN, a general attitude toward the status of women may be discerned only if one accepts a normalized statement. Generally, virtue of women tends to be treasured and guarded, while sexual activity outside strict bounds is disdained. The nature of that disdain and its extent have not yet been fully investigated. Direct comments on the social position and status of women are absent from all our sources, as is discussion of women aberrant from cultural norms. Therefore, it will be necessary to direct our remarks exclusively to Malta, without attempting to extend our conclusions to other parts of the Mediterranean.

Traditionally, women are considered inferior to men in Maltese society. That this is the attitude and firm belief of men is very clear. To women, however, the situation seems to be more closely related to a difference of role than to an acknowledgement of male superiority. Nevertheless, the argument for the subordinate position of women is reinforced in several areas. The Catholic Church, a major influence, teaches that women are morally weak and emphasizes that it was woman who brought about the fall from Paradise. The Maltese civil code, reflecting the teaching of the Church, regards married women as legal minors, not able to administer their own property.[1] The subordination of women is perhaps best illustrated in a fairly common Maltese proverb, "A woman's foot is behind her" (*Il-mara sieqa wara*), that is, her pace is shorter than that of a man, and she is accorded little importance.[2] Less often heard are stronger imprecatory proverbs such as "Seven women in their right senses are surpassed by a mad man" (*Sebgħa nisa f'sensihom miġnun igħaddihom*).[3]

---

* The authors wish to express their appreciation to the Tulane University Research Institute, for a grant to Dr. McLeod, and to the Wenner-Gren Foundation for Anthropology, for a grant to Dr. Herndon, which made the original field research for this paper possible.

[1] Jeremy Boissevain, *Hal Farrug, a Village in Malta* (New York, 1969), chaps. 2–4.
[2] Joseph Aquilina, *A Comparative Dictionary of Maltese Proverbs* (Malta, 1972), xiv–65, 159.
[3] Ibid., xiv–44, 157.

The traditional realm of the woman is the household; that of the man, the field (or the sea) and the marketplace. Although the man is the titular head of the family and is expected to wield the power and make the decisions, the situation is often otherwise. Daily decisions and authority are often in the hands of women. Nor is there a strict division of labor within the household along sexual lines. For example, cooking, though it is usually done by women, is not regarded as "women's work" and may be undertaken by men. The same is true of other work tasks around the house. Nor are women strangers to agricultural or fishing activities; they are often called upon to assist husbands or male relatives in planting, cultivating, or harvesting fields, or in fishing expeditions.

Although the Maltese reckon kin relationships equally through males and females, there tends to be a certain amount of bias in favor of the mother's relatives. This matrilateral bias in an otherwise bilateral kinship system is due to the great strength of the mother-daughter link.[4] The emphasis of the bond between mother and daughter in Malta may be related to the intensity and duration of contact between the two.

Mother and daughter are constant companions. A daughter is taken with her mother to church, to market, and to visit relatives. A good daughter is expected to stay at home and help with household tasks as she gets older, rather than going out of the household to make friends with her peers. After she marries, a daughter has a continuing obligation to help in her mother's household and to return there in case of parental sickness or incapacity. Even in the absence of sickness, a married couple tends to visit the wife's parents more often than they visit the husband's.

A son is encouraged to develop broad interests and to make a wide circle of friends while growing up. He is expected to help with household tasks, but these are usually of a nature that demands energy or strength rather than time or companionship. A father will probably take his sons with him on occasion, but the intensity of contact between father and son is much less than that of mother and daughter. Both mother-son and father-daughter contact tend to diminish and formalize as the child grows up. Thus, the only institutionalized enduring bond is that of mother and daughter. In such a situation, it is not unlikely to expect that this bond will have an effect upon the kinship system.

In the area of courtship and marriage, the traditional practice has been that the boy and girl do not meet one another until the time of their engagement. Courtship, supposedly, took place after the formal engagement and under the watchful eyes of parents. Actually, boys and girls, even those of former generations, did manage to meet one another, particularly on village feast days. Other opportunities for conversation are offered before and after services at church, or at sunset, when boys stroll along the quay or village square with their friends and girls walk with sisters or younger siblings. In some cases, a marriage broker (*huttaba*)[5] was used in the past, but this institution had fallen into disuse by the end of the 1960's.

---

[4] Boissevain, *Hal Farrug*, chap. 2.
[5] Ibid., 31.

Today, courtship ideally follows the traditional pattern. In many instances, however, boys will arrange to meet girls in Valletta, the urban area, and they will date one another for a short while before beginning engagement processes.

Change is taking place in many areas of Maltese life. The experiences of the Maltese in World War II initiated much of the alteration of life style and custom, and the process of change has by now touched many areas of activity, thought, and direction.

The status of women, although still subordinate to that of men in terms of legal rights and public activities, has undergone relatively rapid alteration in the past twenty-five years. It is in the area of dress that this change is most readily apparent. The *għonella*, or *faldetta*, was worn by all Maltese women in public prior to World War II. The garment is black, with a large section of stiffened material covering the head. The effect is to reduce the visibility of the wearer's face and body; this once represented a limited kind of purdah. Unlike the attire of some other Semitic-speaking peoples, however, this garment only shades the face from the sides, and the lower part of the face is uncovered. The *faldetta* may still be seen occasionally on older women, particularly in the metropolitan area. It apparently was the required dress of female members of the oldest Maltese lay apostolate group, MUSEUM (*Magister Unitam Sequatur Evangelium Universus Mundus*),[6] but has been abandoned by younger members in favor of severely tailored calf-length black dresses. The majority of women today favor dresses with skirt lengths below the knee, while some unmarried girls wear clothing copied from Italian, German, or French fashions. In 1969–1970 and 1972, young girls were wearing miniskirts and pants suits.

Alteration in feminine fashions has not been without comment. At least two long ballads, or *fatt*, have addressed themselves to the shameful effects of miniskirts. Comments in the song duel of the men have been numerous, although the subject is not one usually found in casual conversation.

Change is taking place in less apparent areas than dress, too, and with more far-reaching consequences. With the advent of full independence from the British Empire, the Maltese government began a moderately successful policy of attracting industry to the islands. This has meant an opening up of opportunities for women to work on assembly lines. Thus, a few women have been given the opportunity to earn money and to make acquaintances outside family and village circles. More importantly, widows no longer must choose between marrying a male kinsman of their deceased husband and selling sexual favors. The choice between the levirate and prostitution has been widened to include a third possibility, a factory job.

As previously mentioned, the unmarried woman may now have boyfriends and may date before formal engagement. Dating more than one man at a time, however, is not approved of. The woman of today who dates several men at the same time will be accused of prostitution or at best will be the subject of gossip. Although it is not always the case that a "good" woman must see her

---

fiancé only in the chaperoned environment of her family's home or his, this remains the usual practice.

Most women, even today, remain essentially confined to home, family, and village. They socialize with one another during shopping trips made three times a day, in walking to or from church, or in promenades in the village square at sunset. They also visit relatives, attend weddings, funerals, and engagement parties, and go to saints' feast days in other villages with their husbands. If they are not married they go with other women. Church societies for women and girls provide a certain amount of organized companionship and opportunity for social activity in visiting the sick, gathering for prayer or lectures, and repairing church vestments.[7]

Most activities divide along sexual lines. Children in school attend all-male or all-female classes. Men and women sit separately in church, for the most part. Church groups are for either men or women, as are other types of voluntary organizations.

Male social life is centered in the band clubs, bars, and athletic or political clubs. Few women go to any of these places, and even the most daring "modern" husband would rarely consider taking his wife to them. On special occasions, such as village feast days, women may go into these male realms briefly, but they tend, even then, to be seated on chairs placed outside the buildings themselves.

Public musical performances are most often held in bars. The central location for musical events in Malta is the Friend to All Bar, which is also a major "house of prostitution." That this is so severely limits the participation of Maltese women in public musical performance. Any woman who sings in public is thought to be a "prostitute," and she probably is.

The problem of the definition of prostitution, however, prevents much clarification from such a statement. In view of this, it is perhaps best to describe local feelings on the matter. The police recognize three types of "prostitutes," which may be placed into two categories according to type of customer. They speak of bar girls, "real" prostitutes, and house girls; bar girls and "real" prostitutes cater to sailors and tourists in the urban area, while house girls' clients are only Maltese.

Bar girls are mainly found on Straight Street in Valletta, an area known for its bars for Europeans and reputed to be the center of prostitution. Bar girls are not necessarily prostitutes. They sell drinks in clip joints and make late appointments to meet men on a given street corner, taking a cash advance, if possible, for services to be rendered. They usually do not keep these appointments, according to the police. A very few of the bar girls are prostitutes and do meet their clients, but they are extremely choosy as to whom they work for.

The "real" prostitutes generally come out into Straight Street about one o'clock in the morning and wait on corners for men. These are usually young, stylish ladies who charge high prices and take their clients to their own apart-

---

[7] See Boissevain, *Saints*, 20; *Hal Farrug*, 40–41.

ments. They may or may not be married; if they are married, the husband is almost never the pimp, although he is aware of his wife's activities.

Maltese men, with the exception of those who may work in the area, do not frequent Straight Street. Some of the girls are Maltese, but many of the "real" prostitutes are from other countries. The police are aware of their existence and sometimes will send plainclothes officers to survey the area and ascertain current prices; however, few arrests are made.

Both the bar girl and the "real" prostitute conform to usual European categories, but the third type does not. This is the house girl. While a residence is involved, the relationship between the owner of the house and the girls in question is somewhat different.[8] Since any Maltese woman who owns a bar is considered to be aberrant, most are labeled as prostitutes, whether they are or not. Thus, a widow whose husband has owned a bar and who has inherited it from him will automatically change status in the eyes of her neighbors if she chooses to continue to run it. This is true whether she remarries or not. Many bars are merely the carriage room of a house which has been converted to public entertainment. The carriage room, a large front room found in older houses, was formerly used for stabling the horses and storing the carriage; today, it may be used simultaneously as garage and living room. If this room is converted into a bar, the situation is one of a house with a public front. Rooms behind the bar include a kitchen, a courtyard, and a workshop, while sleeping quarters are upstairs. Thus, any such bar that happens to be run by a widow automatically contains all the facilities for a "house," and conversion of the downstairs workshop into a bedroom and bath would insure privacy for the owners of the building while allowing for assignations on the ground floor. In a European house of prostitution, girls would live in and possibly be confined to the premises. In the Maltese "house," there is a stricter division between the public area on the ground floor and the private one on the second floor. Girls may be brought into the bar and may come to one bar regularly to work as prostitutes, but they do not use the upper floor either for a residence or for assignations. Their clients are Maltese men, and the general pattern seems to be that a girl acquires a small number of steady patrons.

Bars where singing takes place are apt to acquire a bad reputation. The upper class believes that singers are a rough lot, who do much more fighting than the average person. This probably was once true, but closer police supervision of folksinging may well have led to the present situation of relative calm in singing bars. The musical form sung by male singers, called *taqbil* (rhyming) or *spirtu pront* (quick spirit; that is, clever thinking), is an improvised form in which each singer tries to outdo the other in subtle insults within a strict musical context. Complex rules have developed to prevent direct insult in any form; great singers will use double entendre and even triple entendre to demolish an opponent. This use of indirect insult greatly reduces the likelihood

[8] See, for comparison, Robbie Davis Johnson, "Folklore and Women: A Social Interactional Analysis of the Folklore of a Texas Madam," JOURNAL OF AMERICAN FOLKLORE, 86 (1973), 211–224.

of a singer becoming angry enough at his opponent to start a fight; however, the police still consider singing bars to be an ever-present threat to the peace. As one policeman put it: "There's not much fighting, but it's like a land mine. It's always possible that something could happen." Seen from the outside, then, a singing bar is potential trouble.

From the inside, however, a singing bar is a coterie of friends who join together in comfortable surroundings to enlarge themselves artistically with song. Because of their fame as improvisers of clever verses, they bring into the bars a group of admirers (*dilettanti*) who drink quietly and enjoy heavy doses of folk music. Singers are experts in the use of proverb, jest, double meanings, and complimentary insults. From time to time, a singer of *fatt*, a long, preconceived form concerned with factual events (usually of a gruesome character), will perform. If two specialists of the *bormliza* are present, they too may sing. The singers' view of the singing bar is one of friendship, artistic beauty, creativity, and music.

Because of the public image of the singers as troublemakers, they are regarded by others as unusual, different, and in some ways aberrant. This produces a common association in a singing bar of prostitutes, singers, and homosexuals. In-group behavior prevents the three types of persons from interfering with one another. It is common to find two men holding hands and kissing in one corner, while singers battle out a fine philosophical subject and a prostitute meets a customer in the back room. Although not every singing bar conforms to this definition, the largest "house" does.

The owner is Mary,[9] the widow of a singer who bought the bar for the benefit of music. When he died, his singer friends helped his widow keep the business afloat. This was some years ago; but it is not uncommon to wander into Mary's in the afternoon and find a singer retiling the kitchen floor or fixing the plumbing. Mary is said to be "in concubinage" with one male singer. She seems not to give favors to any other men. For busy weekend nights she usually has one or two girls who spend the evening in the bar, drinking tea or soft drinks and occasionally disappearing.

A man who wishes to avail himself of one of the girls will buy a round of drinks for the house, disappear, and later reappear. Each girl describes these men as "boyfriends," and they seem to be very few in number. Individual girls do not stay long in one "house"; in three to six months, a new girl will have replaced the previous one. A girl's "boyfriends" follow her from bar to bar. Her small children, if she has any, often accompany her to the bar and may play in the bar area. A girl's husband will sometimes come to the bar but usually does not stay long; he always maintains a public stance of ignorance of his wife's activity.

Only a small percentage of the girls who work in "houses" are married. All, including those who marry, have multiple male friends who see to their upkeep throughout their lifetimes. As pointed out previously, most of these young women were widowed early in life and chose not to marry a kinsman of their

---

[9] Names have been changed in an effort to protect individual identities.

deceased husband; total operation of the levirate becomes very difficult in a monogamous society.

It is fairly clear that these girls are not prostitutes in the European sense; nor are they really concubines.[10] Mary herself is perfectly acceptable, but the girls who work out of her house are not. We were gently told that one of them, the great *bormliza* singer, would not be coming to our house with the other musicians on a festive occasion. When we personally invited her to our home, she replied, "No. I cannot come, because I respect you." This is typical; these women never go to the homes of other singers or of their supporters, and, if they chance to meet someone they know from a singing bar in the streets of a village, they do not speak. Such women are regarded as aberrant in Maltese society, both by themselves and others.

The female "public" singers have liaisons with one or more of the male musicians. Ċetta, now sixty-eight, who is acknowledged to be the best of the female singers, has had half a dozen regular clients for some thirty to forty years, all of whom are highly ranked singers. As mentioned above, Mary has a liaison with one singer.

Women who sing in public are not bar girls or street walkers. Their sexual clientele is exclusively Maltese, and limited to from one to ten regular customers.

The style in which these women sing is called the *bormliza*. The *bormliza* is an impromptu haiku-like sung poem, one of the oldest forms of Maltese music, according to informants. Its antiquity is somewhat supported by its clearly Arabic aspects:

(1) melisma, the use of several tones sung to one syllable of text, often employing non-Western pitch relationships;

(2) generally falling melodic contour, starting with a high pitch and going down;

(3) very tight voice type, involving straining of throat muscles and controlled use of diaphragm muscles to produce a very loud sound. (See Appendix I, Example 1.)

These aspects suggest that this is a tradition which possibly dates from the Arab occupation of the islands between the ninth and eleventh centuries. There is no firm proof of this, however. If the form does date from the Arab occupation, it has certainly been altered by the use of three guitars for accompaniment, a practice that tends to force the *bormliza* into the realm of Western tonality.

As is common in all Maltese folk music, two of the three guitarists play an accompaniment pattern (see Appendix I, Example 2). The remaining guitarist plays the same accompaniment pattern while the singers are singing and improvises a melodic segment between parts of a song as well as between songs.

The word *bormliza*, according to folk etymology, comes from Bormla, the old name still in use among many people for the village of Cospicua. A story often repeated is that *bormliza* was originally for women only and that the women of Bormla would sing it while washing their clothes. The suggestion

---

[10] Hence, the quotation marks around *prostitute*—for various usages and terms see Fernando ᵀenriques, *Prostitution and Society* (New York, 1962).

is made that the style developed as a result of sung discussions between women who had congregated, as they still do in many villages, in the village square to wash clothes. In actuality, the account most often heard dates from a performance staged in recent years by two women, Cetta and Mary, although there is some evidence that singing to one's neighbor in an adjoining courtyard or at a nearby washtub has long been a common practice. There is no evidence, however, that the form was ever restricted to women only.

An alternate name for the *bormliza* is *għanja fil-għolli* (song in the high register). This name belies the idea that this type of song was for women only. When men sing *bormliza*, they sing in the female vocal register. When women sing *bormliza*, they sing in the normal mezzo-soprano range. Thus, if the *bormliza* is called "song in the high register," this is clearly a reference to singing by men, in the high tenor range without obligatory use of falsetto. Women who sing do not consider the range to be high.

According to Maltese singers, the *bormliza* was once much more popular than it is today as a folksong form. Many singers of forty years ago could and did sing it. Today, only a few remain who know the intricate rules and possess the magnificent voice required by the form. The impact of the *bormliza* lies both in the words and in the melismatic intricacies of its presentation, and the Maltese require of the *bormliza* singer a full voice capable of sustaining long phrases. This is not at all a prerequisite for *spirtu pront* and is much less important to the singer of *fatt*.

The *bormliza* may be sung as a solo but is properly for two people, who alternate phrases of music. Several forms are considered to be correct. Each song is only one verse in length. In each form of *bormliza*, the song is divided into two parts. The first part has no name, but the second part is called the *gadenza* or *gadanza* (cadenza). The unnamed first part of the *bormliza* is often set. There are perhaps one hundred short verses, which are heard again and again, constituting a standard opening of a song in this style. For example, the first singer might say, "I am going to try my voice," or "I will try to sing," or "We will see if we can sing," as an opening line of the first song. Alternately, a singer might compliment the voice or face of the other singer, or mention love or the nature of life. To use one of these standard opening lines is not obligatory, but deviation from the traditional set is uncommon. The second section, the *gadenza*, is improvised by the singers.

In the first type of *bormliza*, each of the two singers sings one line, and then each repeats his original line. This constitutes the first section. The poetic form is a, b, a, b. Following this, in the *gadenza*, each singer sings two lines. These two lines are used for each singer's personal, improvised comment. The total form of a *bormliza*, then, is a, b, a, b, c, d; parts c and d each are two lines long, and the final word of both c and d must rhyme with the last word of b.

A typical *bormliza* of this type is as follows:

> Singer A:
> *jiena sejjer għanja ngħanni*
>   I am going to sing a song

Singer B:
jiena sejjra nirrispondik
I am going to answer you

Singer A:
jiena sejjer ghanja nghanni
I am going to sing a song

Singer B:
jiena sejjra nirrispondik
I am going to answer you

Singer A:
Rabbi l-kuragg taqtax qalbek
fejn tixbalja irregik
Have courage, don't lose heart
Where you make mistakes, I will correct you.

Singer B:
Naf li ghandek qalbek tajjba
u ghalhekk lijlek nikkuntentik.
I know you have a good heart
And for that I will make you happy.

In the second type of *bormliza*, each singer sings the same two lines in the first part, then repeats them. Thus, in the first section, the same two lines are heard four times. Then each singer has two lines of his own in the *gadenza*. One of the typical *bormliza* used for ending a set or saying goodbye is of this type:

Singer A:
Ta l'ahhar il bonasijra
Ghax sar il-hin
It is the last goodnight
Because for us the time is ripe

Singer B:
Ta l'ahhar il bonasijra
Ghax sar il-hin

Singer A:
Ta l'ahhar il bonasijra
Ghax sar il-hin

Singer B:
Ta l'ahhar il bonasijra
Ghax sar il-hin

Singer A:
Darb' ohra nargghu niltaqghu
'K ahna nibqghu mal-hajjin
Another time we will meet
If we are still among the living

Singer B:

Kemm qiegħed jiddispjeċini
Għax sa niġu mifrudin
How sad I am
Because we are going to part.

In the third type of *bormliza*, a single individual answers himself. The form employed may be either of the two above.

The *bormliza* is an extremely demanding style, because it requires tremendous vocal power and control. As phrases are extremely long, lung power and breath control are essential. Most singers admit that they do not sing this style because they do not have enough vocal power to sustain these short, poignant songs. The words are simple; the melismatic nature of the style demands vocal agility and endurance that few possess. Of those who attempt the style, few are able to succeed.

Those who do sing *bormliza* will usually sing more than one at a given time. In a typical performance, six or more *bormliza* are sung. The guitarists vamp from the end of one song to the beginning of another, as if stringing pearls together with their music.

Perhaps the most important aspect of the *bormliza* is the haiku-like quality of the poetry. Each song is a tiny, short statement of a subject, distilled until it shines with a perfection unlike any other. It represents an opportunity for the miniaturist musicians to speak. Since the first part is often standard, only the second section reflects the thinking of the singer. In two short lines, each singer is given the opportunity to express an entire subject. The result is a poetic form of jewel-like quality. Each singer must complement the other, and the compressed nature of the form gives it an almost romantic quality. The *bormliza* contrasts sharply with the other commonly found Maltese musical styles— both the *spirtu pront* and the *fatt* are much longer. The contrast is greatest in the area of text and subject matter. The following English translation of a text illustrates the possibilities of the *bormliza* form:

A: Where is my voice of yesteryear,
B: of when I was fourteen?
A: Where is my voice of yesteryear,
B: of when I was fourteen?

A: Tell me where it has gone,
   I cannot leave without it.

B: I grow old and fade away like the tide.
   I want to sing; I cannot.

This, then, is the type of song used by those women who sing in the public arena in Malta. The women who sing *bormliza* are "prostitutes." They sing with men or with other women in the bars and houses of "prostitution."

Women who sing in the private arena, however, use other styles of singing. We mentioned earlier the story of women singing *bormliza* with one another while washing clothes. This does happen; however, the style used by these women is *spirtu pront*, the song-duel style, and not *bormliza*. The context is not the village washing place. It is one woman—in one courtyard—singing to another woman—in another courtyard. Neither personal linen nor sung insults are aired in public.

A ploy sometimes used is for a woman to compose a verse of *spirtu pront* and send one of her children to the roof of the house to sing it at a neighboring woman when the latter is in her courtyard. The neighbor may reply in song; more usual, however, is a reaction of anger and a like response through the neighbor's children. This provides an opportunity for indirect insult; the children are not blamed, but they are provided with an opportunity to learn and practice a form they may sing later in other contexts.

In addition to this direct or indirect song duelling, which in any case is hoped by the participants to be anonymous, women do get together for *xalati*, a kind of bus picnic. On a *xalata*, women hire a bus and driver, and often a male guitarist (since few women play the guitar). Piling box lunches (rabbit stew, bread, fruit), small children, wine, and themselves into the bus in the afternoon, they then spend twelve or more hours driving around Malta, singing standard verses and snatches of song duels they have heard on the radio or on tape. With the exception of a few standard comments to a bad bus driver, these verses are not insulting and are not intended to be. Most often, they do not rhyme properly (a, b, c, b) and do not follow in any sequence or on any particular subject, so that they bear very little resemblance to the song duel engaged in by the men.

Although the younger "prostitutes" are said to organize *xalati*, during which they sing dirty songs, we do not have any evidence of this at the present time. Local gossip has it that this is the favored recreation of these women on Sundays (their day off).

In Malta, the contrast is clear. Women who sing in public are regarded as "prostitutes"; women who are not prostitutes do not sing in public places (that is, with an audience). Women who sing in public sing *bormliza*; women who do not sing in public sing a version of the song duel. Women who sing in public may sing with other women, alone, or with men; women who sing in private direct their messages at another woman, whether they sing the verses themselves or have a child—who may be male or female, but is usually male— sing the song for them.

There is a dualism here which can, perhaps, be summarized by the following series of related fundamental oppositions operant in traditional Maltese culture:

>Public : Private
>Men's realm : Women's realm
>Outer world : Inner world (home, family)
>Conflict/insult : Peace/compliment

It is the prostitute who sings *bormliza* who forms the point of articulation between the two sets of oppositions. It is in her singing of the *bormliza* that elements of compliment appear in the public, men's realm of the bar, for example. If a woman sings *bormliza* alone, with another woman, or with a man, compliments and other comments are direct; there are no insults. If, however, a man sings *bormliza* with another man (a rare situation), the compliments are, through use of double entendre, really insults.[11] In addition, the woman who sings in public is invading the men's realm, the outer world.

We could probably also make a case for the opposition of night and day—night : male : : day : female. It is generally thought that a good woman stays home after dark, while the night is the time men gather in bars and clubs. Thus, the woman who appears in a bar or club at night is crossing a set of subtle cultural divisions.

It is clear that as long as social forces are in play, a norm can be established; however, in areas within a society which are accepted as aberrant, a certain amount of structural blurring takes place. In the Maltese case, this might be considered as a mark of the liminality of the prostitute. As the prostitute's role is considered to be aberrant, so the symbols and the structural principles involved in her art form might be expected to shift from the norm into a metaphorical statement that differs markedly from expression of the same art form in a different context or with different social positions of the singers involved.

It is interesting to note that the *bormliza*, said to be the oldest musical form on Malta, is retained by the "prostitute" rather than by the more conservative women or men of the mainstream of Maltese life. Our assumption has always been, in Western culture, that prostitution as a way of life is a form of deviant behavior. We have also made the assumption that whatever is a clear retention of the past is an item of value, which has been preserved in order to revitalize culture in a time of change. The *bormliza* is a good candidate for such an assumption; the beauty of the verse, the starkness of the poetry, the incredible strength and agility required to sing it, all smack of values that any culture might wish to preserve.

It is also clear that the Maltese themselves appreciate and value the *bormliza*. Those who still sing it are regarded as somewhat superhuman, and other singers try to help older *bormliza* singers to create new and even more beautiful verse endings. For the master singer of the island, a group of *bormliza* is like a string of pearls, and even the foreigner cannot help but be caught up in the atmosphere these songs create. Yet the form is preserved by "prostitutes."

Perhaps it is necessary to reconsider our assumption that prostitution is always regarded as deviant, despite the fact that it is regarded as somewhat aberrant even by those women who are Maltese "prostitutes." However, much as the Maltese pattern of "prostitution" may be considered to be deviant, or an unacceptable, negatively sanctioned alternative to the levirate, until recently it has been the only alternative. Structurally, our analysis of Maltese music or of Maltese fundamental oppositions would be much neater without considering the "prostitute."

The fact remains, however, that there is a blending of structural oppositions

---

[11] See Marcia Herndon and Norma McLeod, "The Use of Nicknames as Evaluators of Personal Competence in Malta," *Texas Working Papers in Sociolinguistics*, 14.

in the "prostitute"; there is a musical form that owes much of its survival to these women. Perhaps, since prostitution is usually considered to be the oldest profession, there may be some justice in the association.

The form seems to be dying, however. We might well wish to take the point of view that this can be explained by the very fact that it is being sustained and sung by liminal figures. Certainly, economic and social changes in Malta, too, will have an effect on the context and world view of all those involved in music, as well as prostitution.

APPENDIX I

Musical Examples

Example 1. *Bormliza* by two singers

Example 2. Accompanying guitar pattern

APPENDIX II

Text of Musical Example

Singer A:

U minn dit-trieq għaddejt u ngħaddi
Għax dit-trieq passi tal-ħlewwa

I traveled and will retravel this street
Because this street is a passage of sweetness

Singer B:

U minn dit-trieq għaddejt u ngħaddi
Għax dit-trieq passi tal-ħlewwa

Singer A:

U minn dit-trieq għaddejt u ngħaddi
Għax dit-trieq passi tal-ħlewwa

Singer B:

U minn dit-trieq għaddejt u ngħaddi
Għax dit-trieq passi tal-ħlewwa

Singer A:

U inti dritt taqsamli l-qalbi
U tkun fil-bieb tidhol il-ġewwa

(And) straight away you break my heart;
When you stand in the doorway, you come in.

Singer B:

Jiena miegħek imxejt ta' mara
U, jien, u jien, ma mxejt bid-dnewwa

I kept my word as a woman with you;
And I was never cruel.

APPENDIX III

Musical Conventions Used

♪ = grace note before the beat

♪ = grace note on the beat

∧ = very hard accent

♩ = pitch approx. one quarter tone above

ʄ = pitch unclear

, = slight catch breath

\ = voice glides down

/ = voice glides up

∧ = voice glides up then down

R = rasp in the voice

GR470
W65

$770500031

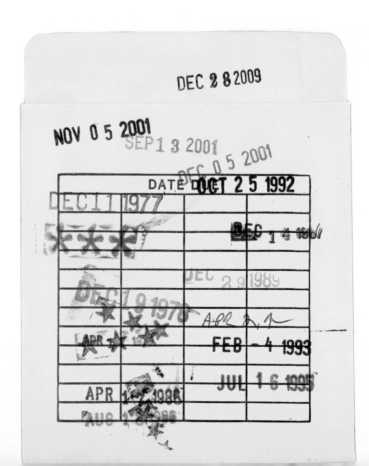